MAKING QUALITY HAPPEN

TED COCHEU

MAKING QUALITY HAPPEN

HOW TRAINING CAN TURN STRATEGY INTO REAL IMPROVEMENT

Jossey-Bass Publishers • San Francisco

Substantial discounts on bulk quantities of Jossey-Bass books are available to corporations, professional associations, and other organizations. For details and discount information, contact the special sales department at Jossey-Bass Inc., Publishers. (415) 433-1740; Fax (415)433-0499.

For sales outside of the United States, contact Maxwell Macmillan International Publishing Group, 866 Third Avenue, New York, New York 10022.

Manufactured in the United States of America

10% POST CONSUMER WASTE

The paper used in this book is acid-free and meets the State of California requirements for recycled paper (50 percent recycled waste, including 10 percent postconsumer waste), which are the strictest guidelines for recycled paper currently in use in the United States.

Library of Congress Cataloging-in-Publication Data
Cocheu, Ted, date.
   Making quality happen : how training can turn strategy into real improvement / Ted Cocheu. — 1st ed.
      p.   cm. — (The Jossey-Bass management series)
   Includes bibliographical references and index.
   ISBN 1-55542-521-6
   1. Employees—Training of.   2. Quality control.   I. Title.
II. Series.
HF5549.5.T7C589   1993
658.3'124—dc20
                                                                92-40200
                                                                CIP

FIRST EDITION
HB Printing   10 9 8 7 6 5 4 3 2 1   *Code 9319*

THE JOSSEY-BASS
MANAGEMENT SERIES

CONTENTS

PREFACE

AS THE CHALLENGE of improving product quality and customer service looms ever larger for all organizations, so does the challenge of giving people the knowledge and skills they need, when they need them, to initiate changes. Quality requires improvement, improvement means change, and change is enabled by gaining and applying new attitudes, knowledge, and skills.

In his article "Making It Happen," Tom Peters insists that "workforce training must become a corporate (and indeed a national) obsession. . . . It is on this variable that the outcome of the overall competitive struggle may most strongly depend." Daniel Kim, of the Sloan School of Management at the Massachusetts Institute of Technology, stresses that "how quickly an organization can adapt to the changes dictated by its environment or initiate changes of its own is largely dictated by the organization's ability to learn" (Kim, 1990).

Anyone who doesn't believe Peters and Kim should listen closely to David Kearns, former CEO of Xerox Corporation, which won the Malcolm Baldrige National Quality Award: "Over three or four years we spent about $125 million on quality training. The top twenty-five people in the company pounded out the initial decision to go after quality, . . . and training was the absolute underpinning of it" (Galagan, 1991a).

Perhaps Japanese quality expert Kaoru Ishikawa best summed up the idea when he said that quality "begins with education and ends with education" (1985, p. 3).

Just knowing that training is important isn't enough. Training must also be effective. Hordes of people have descended on hundreds of quality-related seminars over the last few years, and there is growing concern that companies may not be getting all the bang they had bargained for from their training buck.

A recent study of five hundred American manufacturing and service companies, published in the *Economist,* found that "only a third felt their total quality programs were having a 'significant impact' on their competitiveness" ("Cracks in Quality," 1992). A new study by A. T. Kearney of more than one hundred British companies, noted in the same article, showed that a disappointingly low one in five believed that their quality programs had produced "tangible results."

A significant reason for this failure has been the tendency of companies to begin quality-related training before establishing an overall strategy for improvement. Training in the absence of strategy is a blunt weapon in the battle for quality.

Background

The idea for this book evolved from my experience as a quality consultant. I was asked to work with a company that was coming under increasing pressure from its largest industrial customers to put a total quality management program in place. In his rush to be responsive, the new president directed the quality assurance and training departments to start training people throughout the organization in the full spectrum of relevant subjects. Everybody was supposed to get a brief exposure to quality awareness training. People in the factory were to be trained in statistical process control. Engineers were exhorted to become proficient in statistical design of experiments. People in purchasing were to be taught how to manage suppliers, and so on.

On the face of it, the plan seemed to make sense. Doing things differently requires new knowledge and skills, and training seemed like a good place to start. When people's training records were examined, however, it became clear that training alone was not the solution. In fact, much of the quality training had already taken place over the preceding three years, and the company had made little tangible progress.

This finding presented the president with a dilemma. He needed to take immediate action to demonstrate to customers how committed the company was to quality. The simplest and quickest way was to put people into classrooms and report training statistics. But this method had not worked before, so why would it work this time? What could he do? What had been missing before?

What had been missing was an understanding that quality improvement requires fundamental organizational change and that change requires commitment, leadership, and strategy. The company needed a strategy for change and improvement to give context, direction, and purpose to the training. Once established, training could prepare people to learn, change, and improve in the pursuit of the company's quality objectives. This realization crystallized the two key points that now underlie all of my quality training efforts: strategy must precede training, and training must be specifically focused to facilitate the implementation of strategy.

From this early work evolved the six-step improvement strategy and the six-phase training curriculum that are the subjects of this book. One strategic step lays the groundwork for the steps that follow, and each phase of training lays a foundation of knowledge, skills, and attitudes on which later phases build.

As people are able to learn and change, they create the capacity for the organization to change. As that capacity develops, the organization can realize significant improvements. In this book, my purpose is to help organizations of every size and type avoid the false starts and resulting frustrations that so many others have experienced in their pursuit of quality. I want to cast light on the path of improvement and provide simple direction for travelers on what has become a confusing journey.

Is This Book for You?

Every successful quality effort I have seen over the last decade has been undertaken by a few people with vision, brave individuals who knew at a gut level that the status quo would not be good enough for the future. People ultimately emerge from within the organization to begin breaking the ground for change. Often that ground is hard and barren; occasionally, however, it is fertile and ready for sowing. Sometimes the area to be plowed encompasses the entire organization, sometimes only a department. No matter how broad or narrow the scope, improvement begins with the deep-felt commitment of individuals to change for the better the circumstances in which they find themselves.

Making Quality Happen was written for advocates of change, regardless of where in the organization they may find themselves. Ideally, the quality spark ignites in the executive suite and then the fire spreads throughout the company. But change can begin wherever it is most deeply felt. I have seen leadership for improvement successfully emerge from just about every department, from manufacturing to quality control to sales to human resources. It can come from vice presidents, directors, managers, or individual contributors. Regardless of your title or function, if you are committed to overcoming the stubborn inertia of business as usual and want to get the improvement process rolling, this book is for you.

This book is also a resource for consultants, trainers, organizational developers, and other professionals charged with implementing quality training in the organizations they support. Too often the tendency for staff specialists is to bow to the will of line managers who seem convinced that they know best what to do. In truth, however, leadership on the "soft side" of quality must be an essential countervailing force in a business environment often dominated by the technically and financially minded. I hope to provide reinforcement to those who know that, in the rush for quality, people must come first and to encourage them to hold to their convictions when the stampede begins.

New initiates to quality management, as well as war-torn veterans, are buffeted by a blizzard of three-letter acronyms: TQM, TQC, SPC, DOE, QFD, QCC, and so on. The equally long litany of related training programs has resulted in unnecessary confusion and frustration. Training for quality is an expensive proposition, and people are looking for practical, cost-effective approaches that they can adapt to meet the needs of their organizations. This is a book for busy people who want solutions, not theories. It organizes a lot of firsthand knowledge and experience from top-notch companies into a simple-to-use approach. It makes sense of the jargon, tools, and techniques and puts them into a sequenced curriculum of courses that will help move any organization into a stronger competitive position.

What's Different About This Book?

There are so many books these days on quality, what makes this one different? Four attributes distinguish this book from the many colorful covers that might catch the reader's eye in the local bookstore. *Making Quality Happen* reveals

• *How to make training effective:* Training is usually the single most expensive and time-consuming activity in the initial stages of a quality program, and this is the first book completely dedicated to training for quality. It is the single source of guidance on structuring training, for every topic from quality awareness and team skills to quality management systems and advanced methods.

• *How it all fits together:* The literature on quality is replete with lists of ingredients for quality: listen more closely to customers, encourage employee involvement, move from inspection to prevention, implement statistical process controls, and so on. What is missing for the practitioner trying to improve quality is the recipe—how to actually put it all together and start making the transition, step by step. In what sequence should things be done? How do all the components fit together? How do you keep the cart from getting in front of the horse? The six-step quality strategy and the six-phase training curriculum provide the much-needed sequencing.

- *How training integrates with strategy:* Companies have traditionally focused their initial quality efforts and related training on one or more of three areas: quality awareness, employee involvement, and statistical process control. But awareness, involvement, and statistics by themselves cannot bring about significant, continual improvement. What is needed is all three of these, and much more, organized in such a way that training supports the implementation of a comprehensive improvement strategy. The guiding principle here is that training is effective only if it facilitates the implementation of strategy. Anything less leads to disappointment and wasted resources.

- *How to develop the organization by developing people:* Improvement, by definition, means change. What is often overlooked in training programs is that the ability of organizations to develop and change is regulated by the development of people's capability to do the same. People's learning must parallel the unfolding of the organization's improvement strategy. Progress cannot be made any more quickly than people can internalize new attitudes, knowledge, and skills. The sequence of the six phases of training presented here is designed to facilitate the organization's orderly progress along the path of improved quality.

Overview of the Contents

The first chapter examines the importance of creating an overall improvement strategy and demonstrates how training must be positioned to support it. A proven and flexible strategy for improvement is provided, which shows where, when, and how training fits in. Chapter One describes what must be done to improve quality and establishes the context for the succeeding chapters. Chapters Two through Seven describe each of the six training phases in detail, showing what kind of training is needed at every level of the organization, when it is needed, and how people can acquire the relevant concepts, techniques, and skills.

The first phase of training involves executives in the process of learning how to build a leadership foundation for improvement. Chapter Two begins by acknowledging the many dilemmas encountered in attempting to educate executives and shows how to avoid or overcome the obstacles. A simple four-session series is presented that helps executives learn in a comfortable way and enables them to complete the first two steps in the improvement strategy. Completing these two steps, preparation and planning, establishes the foundation on which the entire improvement process is built.

Chapter Three describes the training needed to gain the understanding and commitment of people throughout the organization. The main objective of this second phase of training is to communicate the elements of the foundation built by executives in the first phase, including quality assessment, vision, philosophy, strategy, goals, and the plan. Different approaches are shown for training managers and individual contributors, who have different roles and responsibilities.

The third phase of training, discussed in Chapter Four, focuses on building a quality management system, which can provide the framework needed to support the organization's improvement efforts. Many organizations use the criteria defined in quality standards and awards, such as the International Standards Organization (ISO) 9000 Series, the Malcolm Baldrige National Quality Award, the Deming Prize, and the President's Award for Quality and Productivity Improvement, as a starting point for their quality management systems. The particular system an organization chooses to implement depends on its specific needs and objectives, but all the systems require training people in all departments.

Chapter Five, which covers the fourth training phase, describes how to empower improvement teams, deploy quality strategy within the organization, and train people to work collectively toward quality goals. Different approaches are recommended for team members, team leaders, and managers. The training in teamwork that everyone needs includes empowerment, meeting management, problem-solving and decision-making skills, as well as the use of the basic quality tools. Special additional training is required for team leaders and managers. The skills needed to establish effective teamwork are a prerequisite to implementing statistical process control and the other more advanced quantitative methods.

The fifth phase of training, discussed in Chapter Six, addresses the improvement of production and business processes. All repetitive work can be broken down into processes; and understanding, controlling, and improving those processes is the heart of quality. The chapter begins with an explanation of the four key concepts underlying all process management tools and continues with descriptions of how to teach and apply the techniques of statistical process control and business process improvement. Structured models are provided to guide training in and use of both techniques.

Chapter Seven explores the sixth phase, which involves methods for creating a learning organization—that is, an organization that enables people to make learning a lifelong endeavor. Continual improvement means continual change, which requires constant learning. When the walls between quality training and other training functions are broken down, people can more readily see how all learning resources and opportunities ultimately support the goal of quality. Organizations must help people develop the ability to teach one another, so that learning can become a more natural, spontaneous activity. New, more advanced quality techniques can also be explored as people learn to master the basics. Parallel to developing an improvement strategy, each organization needs to foster a learning strategy. Such a strategy will help people learn more from their everyday experiences, question assumptions that retard progress, and take advantage of the unlimited learning resources available to us all.

Acknowledgments

Over the years, the people who have most encouraged me to write have been the members of the editorial staff of the American Society for Training and Development. By publishing my articles and including me in their editorial activities, Ellen Carvevale, Pat Galagan, Diane Kirrane, and Nancy Olsen have given me the opportunity and confidence to share my experiences with the broader professional community. Without that opportunity, I would not have written this book.

My many associates at Conner Peripherals have been very patient and supportive of this project, which has consumed my time for the past eighteen months. Harvey Kroll, my boss and good friend, has given me the freedom to carve out precious periods of time from my job to write and to refine my thinking. He has been more than generous in supporting professional activities that have taken me around the country in order to talk to and learn from colleagues and fellow practitioners. With his help, I have been able to have my cake and eat it too: work at a great company like Conner and complete this book, which has been so important to me. And my conceptual understanding of quantitative methods has increased, thanks to the patient mentoring of our company statistician, Thanh C. Tran.

The list of colleagues who have contributed to my thinking for the book and my understanding of quality are many, so I will mention only a few here. Foremost among them is Jim Harrington, currently serving as the international quality adviser to Ernst & Young. He may not even realize the value of the mentoring and professional respect he offered. Those familiar with his work will immediately recognize his influence in such concepts as the improvement process and business process improvement.

My good friend Marc Taylor can always be counted on to be a creative support and a sounding board for my half-baked ideas. I feel that our relationship is living proof of synergy, since I always come away from our conversations with more than either of us imagined possible. Jerry deJaager continues to provide a unique perspective that I find refreshing, and his no-holds-barred feedback is rare and valuable. Sara Zeff's candid critique of an early draft helped me overcome many of my most troubling writing habits. And the practitioner-centered comments from Craig Hagopian of Epson America and Cathy Feeney of Owens and Minor helped focus and reinforce many key points.

Although I would like to say that it was my idea, I must credit the editors at Jossey-Bass with the original idea for *Making Quality Happen*. They spotted my quality training article in *Training & Development* and believed in me enough to ask me to write a book about my thoughts and experiences. Most recently, Sarah Polster has helped shape the manuscript into a work worthy of publication, although all its limitations are solely my responsibility.

Saving the best for last, I cannot say enough about how important the support, involvement, and encouragement of my wonderful wife, Susan Lester, have been to this book, as well as to my life in general. She read and reread each wretched draft of the manuscript and made it better with her every touch. And she said nothing as our private lives were put on hold for over a year while I spent all my weekends and holidays working on the book.

To Susan and all my friends and colleagues who made the book possible, thank you. I hope that I can someday repay your generosity.

Los Gatos, California   Ted Cocheu
January 1993

THE AUTHOR

TED COCHEU is director of organizational development for Conner Peripherals, which was ranked by *Fortune* magazine in 1989 as America's fastest-growing manufacturing corporation. He received his B.A. degree (1972) in sociology and his M.A. degree (1976) in public policy from the University of California, Santa Barbara.

Before joining Conner, Cocheu worked as a private consultant in the fields of quality improvement, management and organizational development, and design of training systems. He served as a consultant to Fortune 500 clients in industries as diverse as electronics, medical instruments, natural resources, and insurance. His quality consulting tasks ranged from strategic quality planning and employee opinion surveys to curriculum development and instruction. Cocheu's work in quality began in 1981, when he designed and delivered a corporate quality training program to managers throughout the United States and Europe. Before working as a consultant, he was a training and development manager for several multinational electronics firms.

Cocheu has written numerous articles on the subjects of quality, training, and human resource management. His work has been published in such professional journals as *Quality Progress, Training & Development, Technical & Skills Training,*

Training Magazine, and *Design & Construction Quality Forum.* Cocheu is a frequent speaker on training for quality at regional and national conferences. He has served as chapter president for the American Society for Training and Development, is on the editorial review board for *Training & Development,* and is a member of the American Society for Quality Control.

MAKING
QUALITY
HAPPEN

1

Putting Strategy Before Training

"THE REASON WHY success-ful quality companies were successful is that they had good management vision and strategies in addition to their commitment to quality," says Procter & Gamble CEO Edwin Artzt (Bemowski, 1992). The strategy chosen by management provides the direction and structure people need to go about the improvement process. Training can communicate that strategy throughout the organization, help overcome resistance to change, and provide the knowledge and skills people need to proceed (Cocheu, 1992a).

Effective training specifically supports the organization's improvement strategy. When it does, training is a powerful tool to facilitate the implementation of strategy. Although it can foster motivation and develop knowledge and skills, training can only be effective if what is learned can be applied on the job and is consistent with how management runs the business. "The key thing about training is that it should integrate," says former Xerox CEO David Kearns. "The strategy of the company, the direction of the company, the vision of the company, and the skills and behavior that people need in order to get the job done should all be combined and integrated into the training. That's the key thrust I'd like to see" (Galagan, 1991a). Strategy is the subject of this first chapter because so many

1

organizations overlook this simple truth: strategy must precede training.

Since broad-scale training of the work force is known to be essential in any improvement effort, and is also the simplest and most visible activity to organize, many well-intentioned companies kick off their quality campaigns with extensive training programs. The problem comes when people get back to their jobs after training and realize that nothing has really changed, that what they learned sounded good in the classroom but will not be supported or applied back at work. Training can actually cause more damage than good in these cases. If it falsely raises people's expectations about change and leads to disappointment, it further hardens their skeptical attitudes about management's commitment to improvement.

Yves Van Nuland, quality manager with a Belgian chemical company, watched the company conduct training in the absence of strategy. When the initial enthusiasm for the quality program began to wane, the general manager decided that additional training was needed. All two hundred staff members were required to attend a quality seminar. "Reactions [to the training] were strongly divided. Once again, due to the lack of strategy and well defined plan, people were very critical. The translation of training to the work place once again failed" (Van Nuland, 1990).

"To have long-lasting positive results, training should first be understood as part of an organization's strategic plan," according to consultant Nina Fishman (1990). The plan must "indicate that if the organization is to remain competitive, all its employees need to acquire core competencies in quality improvement."

Although specific improvement strategies vary greatly from company to company, the successful ones follow, in one way or another, a six-step approach: preparation, planning, awareness, deployment, implementation, and continuous improvement (see Figure 1.1).

The way a company adapts the six-step improvement strategy to meet its needs is influenced by the stage of quality it has already achieved. The "stages of quality management matu-

Figure 1.1. Six-Step Improvement Strategy.

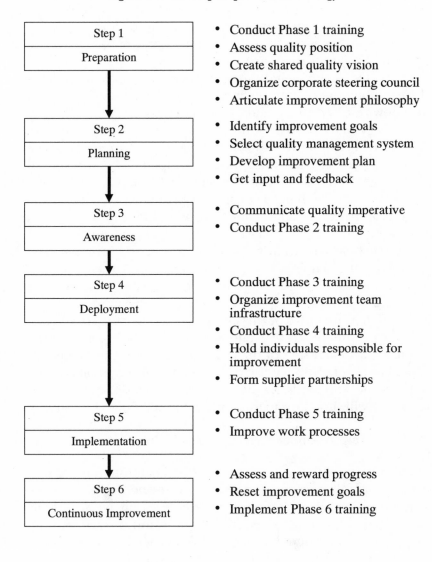

| Step 1
Preparation | • Conduct Phase 1 training
• Assess quality position
• Create shared quality vision
• Organize corporate steering council
• Articulate improvement philosophy |

| Step 2
Planning | • Identify improvement goals
• Select quality management system
• Develop improvement plan
• Get input and feedback |

| Step 3
Awareness | • Communicate quality imperative
• Conduct Phase 2 training |

| Step 4
Deployment | • Conduct Phase 3 training
• Organize improvement team infrastructure
• Conduct Phase 4 training
• Hold individuals responsible for improvement
• Form supplier partnerships |

| Step 5
Implementation | • Conduct Phase 5 training
• Improve work processes |

| Step 6
Continuous Improvement | • Assess and reward progress
• Reset improvement goals
• Implement Phase 6 training |

rity" discussed by Philip Crosby (1979) are uncertainty, awakening, enlightenment, wisdom, and certainty. Most organizations are at the stage of enlightenment, which, according to Crosby, "appears with the decision to go ahead and really conduct a formal, regulation, card-carrying quality improvement program" (p. 29). This stage includes organizations that have made half-hearted but failed attempts in the past to improve quality and are now resolved to try again to make it work.

The first five steps of the improvement strategy shown in Figure 1.1 are designed for "enlightened" organizations as well as those that are still "awakening." Companies floundering in the "uncertainty" stage usually need a precipitating event, such as loss of market share or declining profits, to face up to the quality imperative. Those rare companies that have achieved "wisdom" or "certainty" have already developed much of the infrastructure and training needed to get the improvement process going. Their strategies should reinforce their previous accomplishments and focus on refining their systems and training in the sixth step, continuous improvement.

The remainder of this chapter examines the six steps of the improvement strategy and shows how training fits in (see Figure 1.2). Each step of the strategy builds on the preceding ones, and each phase of the training curriculum builds on the knowledge and skills learned in earlier phases. Subsequent chapters will show how to implement the six phases of training.

Improvement Strategy, Step 1: Preparation

Quality starts with top management and cannot be delegated for one simple reason: leadership cannot be delegated. The degree of success a company will achieve can be accurately predicted by how much executives understand and are committed to the improvement process. A participant in a recent executive seminar remarked, "Quality is one of the few places where the 'trickle-down theory' actually works."

The first step of the improvement strategy, preparation, involves conducting Phase 1 training for executives, assessing the organization's quality position, forming the corporate steering council, and creating a quality vision.

Figure 1.2. Integrated Training Curriculum.

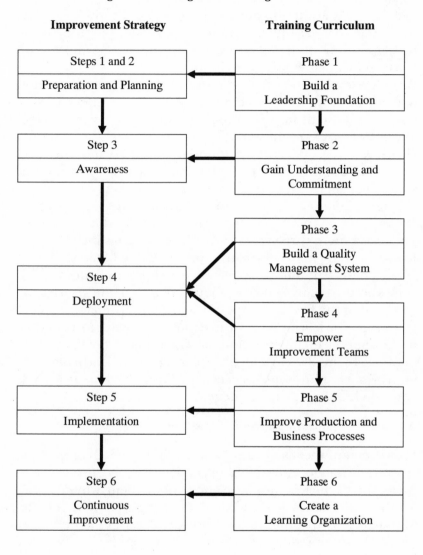

Improvement Strategy

Training Curriculum

| Steps 1 and 2 |
| Preparation and Planning |

| Phase 1 |
| Build a Leadership Foundation |

| Step 3 |
| Awareness |

| Phase 2 |
| Gain Understanding and Commitment |

| Phase 3 |
| Build a Quality Management System |

| Step 4 |
| Deployment |

| Phase 4 |
| Empower Improvement Teams |

| Step 5 |
| Implementation |

| Phase 5 |
| Improve Production and Business Processes |

| Step 6 |
| Continuous Improvement |

| Phase 6 |
| Create a Learning Organization |

Conduct Phase 1 Training (Building a Leadership Foundation)

Quality starts at the top and works its way down the organization, and so must quality training. Although strategy must precede training, the top managers of the organization must learn about quality and how to implement improvement before they can develop the strategy. Fortunately, the need for senior management training is being recognized, as reflected in a quality study of the international computer industry conducted jointly by Ernst & Young and the American Quality Foundation (Ernst & Young, 1992). They found that "the greatest increase in quality training over the next three years is planned for senior management, who will go from the current industrywide average of 15 hours per year to an industrywide average of 26 hours per year" (p. 9). This figure is up from less than ten hours per year a mere three years ago. These averages include data from Canada, Japan, Germany, and the United States.

Phase 1 training is a task-oriented, learning-doing process where executives learn about quality in the process of completing the first two steps of the strategy: preparation and planning. The learning activities enable executives to assess the organization's quality position, create a shared quality vision, organize themselves as a quality steering council, articulate an improvement philosophy, select a quality management system, and develop their goals, strategy, and plan.

Assess the Organization's Quality Position

Improvement means change, and people need a compelling reason to change. After all, if executives have been successful doing things the way they have always done them, why change? The answer comes from what Peter Senge (1990b), of the Massachusetts Institute of Technology, describes as "creative tension": "Creative tension comes from seeing clearly where we want to be, our vision, and telling the truth about where we are, our current reality. The gap between the two generates a natural tension. . . . Creative tension cannot be generated from current reality alone. . . . Vision without an understanding of current reality will more likely foster cynicism than creativity.

The principle of creative tension teaches that an accurate picture of current reality is just as important as a compelling picture of a desired future."

Gaining an accurate picture of current reality begins with an assessment of the organization's quality position. This assessment involves soliciting customer feedback, analyzing the organization's competitive strengths and weaknesses, looking at the internal cost structure, and understanding employees' attitudes and opinions. The insights gained from looking at these four sources of data, juxtaposed with a vision of a preferred future, help stimulate busy executives to refocus their attention on quality.

A good example of how the examination of competitive and cost information helped stimulate a company's pursuit of quality improvement is Xerox, winner of the 1989 Malcolm Baldrige National Quality Award. Xerox president Paul Allaire recounts how Xerox became complacent about the competition because the company had essentially invented, built, and, for so many years, "owned" the copier business:

> In the late 1970s, we started to take a hard look at what we were doing at Xerox and how we run our business. And we started to take an equally hard look at the competition. . . . We were startled at what we found. One of the first things we realized was that our costs were too high—and not just a little too high. In fact, the Japanese were selling their small machines for what it cost us to make ours. We assumed that because the machines were low cost, they were low quality—we were wrong! Then we tried to convince ourselves that they could not be making money. Wrong again! They were profitable. That woke us up in a hurry and we went to work in earnest to begin closing the gaps [Allaire and Rickard, 1989].

This is the kind of analysis that can help executives take the first step toward change: drawing a "clear picture of current reality."

Create a Shared Quality Vision

The second element of the creative tension needed to motivate change is a vision, a compelling picture of a desired future. As Senge (1990b) notes, "the natural energy for changing reality comes from holding a picture of what might be that is more important to people than what is." He goes on to say, "People's natural impulse to learn (and improve) is unleashed when they are engaged in an endeavor they consider worthy of their fullest commitment."

In conducting their extensive study of leadership practices, Jim Kouzes and Barry Posner (1987) were struck by the importance of inspiring a shared vision: "The most important role of visions in organizations is to give focus to human energy. Visions are like lenses. . . . They enable everyone concerned with an enterprise to see more clearly what lies ahead of them. . . . We also refer to this as the Jigsaw Puzzle Principle: it is easier to put the puzzle together if you can see what is on the box cover. . . . The leader's job is to paint the big picture, to give people a clear sense of what the puzzle will look like when everyone has put their pieces together. Visions are the big picture" (p. 98).

Developing the quality vision is a natural next step after assessing the company's position on quality. Executives need only look at what they see in the assessment and ask themselves a series of questions: Do we like what we see? Are our customers completely satisfied? Do we have a clear and maintainable advantage over the competition? Do we operate as efficiently and profitably as possible? Do employees trust management and feel empowered to make changes and improvements? If the answers are all yes, they have little reason to change a winning formula. But if the assessment is not consistent with how executives themselves view the company or how they would like it to be positioned in the marketplace, then it is up to them to create a vision of their preferred future that they can easily communicate to customers, employees, and suppliers.

The importance of articulating a corporate vision was reinforced by a recent survey conducted by the Gauntlet Group (1991). Executives in eighty high-technology companies in northern California were asked "What difficulties does your company have achieving organizational excellence?" The most frequent response was "inadequate vision and strategy." The researchers concluded: "If employees do not understand senior management's vision and are not clear about the exact implementation steps to achieve corporate objectives, there will be a greater percentage of wasted time and efforts. People are much more productive if they can see beyond the immediate task in front of them and understand how their efforts contribute to corporate objectives" (p. 4).

The following vision statement of a leading electronics firm is an example of how to provide a concise, powerful message to the entire organization about management's values and commitment to improvement:

> Our vision is to identify customers' needs sooner and fill them faster than the competition. We will provide:
>
> - Innovative solutions to our customers' requirements
> - More reliable products and better quality services than the competition
> - Higher productivity of people and assets than the competition
> - Continuous improvement in everything we do
>
> Every individual and department on the team has customers—the vision applies to us all.

This vision statement captures the essence of the company's time-to-market business strategy while integrating other issues critical to the company's success: closeness to the customer, innovation, reliability and quality, efficiency, continuous improvement, and teamwork. It combines the spirit of what helped make the company a leader in the past while challenging people to continuously improve in the future. More importantly, the vision defines the broad values and priorities that drive the company's everyday business decisions.

The chairman of a leading consumer electronics firm

reaffirmed his vision of quality after having already demonstrated a deep commitment to improvement over the previous
six years. In a company-wide message he implored: "With a
deep sense of urgency, spread dedication to quality to every
facet of the corporation, and achieve a culture of continual
improvement to assure customer satisfaction. There is only one
ultimate goal: zero defects in everything we do." Such a quality
vision, when supported by strong goals and an effective strategy, can help inspire people and mobilize them to walk down
the path of improvement.

Organize the Corporate Steering Council

After they determine where the company is and where they
want it to go, senior managers must formally organize themselves to direct the improvement process. Normally they would
form an improvement steering council composed of the top
managers of the organization.

The responsibility for directing, supporting, and over-
seeing improvement cannot be delegated: "Senior management has to be committed to change. Without genuine,
hands-on commitment, all attempts at quality improvement
and employee involvement are doomed to failure. And that
commitment must take the form of action, not rhetoric. Our
expression for that at Xerox is that managers must walk like
they talk" (Allaire and Rickard, 1989). The first visible expression of that commitment is active participation on the steering
council. For example, the CEO of Baldrige Award–winning
Motorola personally chairs the company's "quality operating
and policy committee." All-day committee meetings are held
twice every quarter. The agenda starts with an update on the
company's key quality initiatives and proceeds with reports by
major business units on the status of their quality accomplishments and shortfalls.

Articulate a Shared Improvement Philosophy

If the quality vision captures "what we want to become," then
the improvement philosophy embodies "what we value and
how we want to operate." The philosophy is an explicit sum-

mary of the unspoken values and assumptions that guide everyday decisions and actions—including how customers, employees, and suppliers should be treated, how priorities should be set, and how decisions should be made. As Daniel Kim (1990) points out, "TQ [total quality] is both an all encompassing philosophy about the whole enterprise of running the business and a set of statistical tools. . . . Without this philosophy, TQ is reduced to a bag of tools. . . . Without the statistical tools, TQ is nothing more than a guiding light to a goal that offers no help for navigating the terrain. TQ's success lay in linking the lofty goals of management with a set of tools to achieve these goals."

The importance of developing a shared philosophy, or common paradigm, cannot be overstated. Executives often assume they agree on their basic values when they really do not. When they realize they disagree, the natural tendency is to try to ignore their differences. The many mixed messages that ensue from such differences cause confusion and heightened skepticism throughout the organization.

An example comes to mind: the top managers in a multibillion-dollar company did not realize or would not acknowledge that they held conflicting assumptions about quality. Although they unanimously agreed that quality was strategically important to the business, some believed the best approach was tighter supervision and inspection, and others knew that it would require a shift to prevention-oriented methods. In another example, a vice president professed her philosophy of developing "partnerships" with suppliers to improve the quality of incoming materials, while the president was single-mindedly pushing for cost reduction. A coherent approach to improvement is not possible until values and assumptions like these are discussed openly and shaped into a common philosophy that everyone can understand, internalize, and act on.

Improvement Strategy, Step 2: Planning

With the vision, steering council, and philosophy in place, the next step is to plan for improvement. Planning for improvement includes identifying improvement goals, selecting a quality management system, developing the improvement plan, and getting input and feedback on the plan.

Identify Improvement Goals

Levinson and DeHont (1992) of Sierra Semiconductor stress the point that "the failure to achieve quality can be—and usually is—the failure of management to set appropriate goals." Improvement goals are a natural outgrowth of the quality assessment. Goal setting starts with a "gap analysis," defining the discrepancy between the current level of performance and that which is desired or needed to remain competitive. People and organizations need clear, tangible goals to focus their efforts and define progress.

When a leading manufacturing firm asked its major industrial customers what their quality requirements for a particular component would be in three years, there was virtual consensus: all were aiming for no more than two hundred to five hundred defective parts per million (DPPM). The standard performance in the industry at the time was in the tens of thousands of DPPM. The company's average quality level was better than in the industry at large but significantly below what would be required in the future. That customer input helped the company develop a corporate-wide product quality goal that was as simply stated as it was challenging: achieve two thousand DPPM or less within three years. Other important goals were also set for reliability, delivery, and service, but the implications of the two thousand DPPM goal were very clear to everyone. Improvement would have to occur at a much faster rate in the future than it had in the past. Achieving that one goal would require the dedicated and coordinated efforts of everyone in the company—marketing, research and development, product engineering, purchasing, process engineering, production. And it would demand a radical and rapid improvement in quality from the company's suppliers.

A comprehensive set of quality goals was developed in 1990 by a leading maker of personal computers. The goals communicated very clearly to suppliers exactly what the company felt it needed in 1991 to compete effectively. Those goals included

- Establishing a worldwide quality council
- Achieving four thousand DPPM for all products and five hundred DPPM for all new products
- Achieving ISO 9000 quality management system certification (discussed in the next section) for all sites within fifteen to twenty months
- Defining and measuring customer service metrics and achieving 20 percent improvement
- Establishing a rigorous key supplier certification program
- Identifying and measuring key quality indexes in all organizations and making a 20 percent improvement

These goals represent a specific, balanced, and comprehensive approach. They focus on a number of the issues central to any successful improvement effort, including the development of an improvement infrastructure, product quality, customer service, supplier quality, and the establishment of quality indexes throughout the organization.

Select a Quality Management System

Supporting a compelling vision with a set of clear goals provides the direction people need to understand where the company is trying to go. The next question is how all the pieces will fit together. It is addressed through the quality management system (QMS) selected by the steering council. A QMS is a means of integrating all the company's quality improvement activities and tying together such diverse issues as management commitment, quality procedures and results, supplier management, statistical process control, and employee involvement and development.

Robert Peach (1990), an active member of national and international quality standards committees, notes: "I have observed a number of cases in which the lack of a basic quality system was a major contributing factor to the stagnation of progress. . . . These companies seem to have prematurely used (otherwise) effective methods of quality improvement before establishing an effective overall quality system to guide the sustained use of the methods."

The most widely accepted QMS internationally is the ISO 9000 series, developed in 1987 by the International Standards Organization (ISO) of Geneva, Switzerland. It was originally adopted by British companies (as British Standard 5750) as a tool to establish whether suppliers' quality systems were adequate to meet their customers' product and service requirements. A supplier must be successfully audited against the appropriate ISO 9000 standard by a registered auditing organization to be certified as an ISO 9000 supplier.

Another highly regarded QMS, the Malcolm Baldrige National Quality Award, was established in 1988 by the National Institute of Standards and Technology, an agency of the U.S. Department of Commerce. In contrast to ISO 9000, which is a compliance standard that can be used to register any company, a maximum of six applicants are selected each year to be Baldrige Award winners. Increasingly, American companies are using the Baldrige Award's comprehensive assessment criteria as a guide for structuring their improvement efforts, without even intending to apply for the award. In 1990, only ninety-seven companies actually applied for the Baldrige Award, but over 125,000 copies of the application guidelines were distributed. As stated in the *1991 Application Guidelines*, "the purpose of the document is twofold. First, it is designed as a guide for Award applicants. . . . Second, it provides a basis for self-assessment by all U.S. organizations that are pursuing quality excellence" (National Institute of Standards and Technology, 1990, p. 1).

Other quality awards whose criteria can serve as the basis of a QMS include the Deming Prize, NASA Excellence Award for Quality and Productivity, President's Award for Quality and Productivity Improvement, and Healthcare Forum/Witt Commitment to Quality Award.

Develop the Improvement Plan

The third activity in the planning step is developing an improvement plan, which should include sequencing and timing of events. A recent study of Japanese companies conducted by Organizational Dynamics, Inc., found, "to our surprise, one differentiating factor emerged almost immediately: implementation plans. Virtually all of the Deming Prize winners can point to clear, detailed, well-communicated total quality improvement plans, the likes of which are rarely encountered in U.S. or European companies. . . . These total quality improvement plans are bound firmly by time, covering between three and five years, with specific annual themes or objectives. Examples of annual themes include reliability, strengthening vendor partnerships, and cycle time reduction" (Labovitz and Chang, 1990). The researchers go on to point out that the plans of award-winning companies detail four main types of activities: those related to senior management, customer satisfaction, employee involvement, and training.

When developing implementation plans, it is easy to be unrealistic, to want to accomplish too much too soon, thereby setting up the organization for failure. Organizations often wait too long to make the commitment and then feel tremendous pressure to make up lost ground quickly. Typically, quality lingers as a low priority for years, with little progress. At some point, quality issues escalate to such a level that they can no longer be ignored. A diversity of opinions about how to address quality emerges, resulting in confusion and conflict. Consensus about the strategic importance of quality starts to form at the executive level. Panic underlies a new sense of urgency to improve. Frustrated at how much time has passed without progress, the top managers want to proceed immediately and see results instantly. They develop a set of unrealistic goals driven by an even more unrealistic implementation schedule. The rest of the organization, by now also frustrated, becomes even more so by what it properly perceives as an unrealistic plan. People try to do the best they can but feel they are fighting a losing battle. The result is a sense of futility and impending failure. Executives become disenchanted because results do not meet their unrealistic expectations, and they begin to lose confidence and interest in the improvement process. The difficulty of making the process work and the lack of immediate progress reinforces their deep-seated skepticism about the viability of the quality effort.

The way to avoid this unfortunate, all-too-familiar scenario is to have a realistic understanding of what the improvement process involves and how much time is needed to move the strategy ahead step by step. Improving quality is not so much a technical issue as it is social and organizational. A company that has functioned in a certain way for years, possibly from its inception, is not going to change overnight—no matter how strongly we may wish or urge it. Sustained improvement involves overcoming a lifetime of conditioning and creating a new prevention-oriented approach to work. People would prefer to be proud of their work rather than just punch a time clock and collect a paycheck, but they become frustrated by working for years in a system that appears indifferent to quality and hostile to change. The old ways of doing business become deeply ingrained habits that no one in the organization is immune to, least of all top management. Improving quality means broad-based organizational change, and change takes patience, persistence, and the ability to build on incremental successes.

The improvement plan should therefore show how the remaining steps of the strategy will be carried out and provide a clear path from the vision to the goals to the methods of addressing them. As Schaffer and Thompson (1992) emphasize in their critique of "total quality" programs, managers must translate the big picture into "sharp and compelling expectations for short-term achievements." By marrying strategic objectives with short-term improvement projects, "managers can translate strategic direction into reality."

Planning requires a strong sense of direction coupled with knowing the right questions to ask at each step: How and when will the communications and training required in the awareness step take place? In the deployment step, how will the quality infrastructure permeate the organization? What types of teams will be required? How will they be set up and trained? In the implementation step, how will the corporate goals be operationalized at every level of the organization? What training will be required, and when and how should it be delivered? In the continuous improvement step, when can results be expected, and how and to whom should they be reported? What will the mechanism be for periodically evaluating and resetting improvement goals? These are but a few of the many questions that must be addressed in the improvement plan to provide people with the direction they will need to work effectively together toward the organization's goals.

Get Input and Feedback

Although responsibility for company-wide quality planning belongs with top management, it would be foolhardy to plan without input and feedback from others in the organization. It is advisable to involve other key managers and technical contributors throughout the preparation and planning steps, which take place through a series of meetings over a period of weeks or months. Broader organizational involvement helps ensure that all important data and points of view are considered and increases the feeling of "ownership" for the results. Getting feedback should be an iterative process, similar to what the Japanese call "catchball," where executives solicit input, consider it in their decision making, ask others to review their preliminary thinking, receive constructive feedback, and consider the feedback before finalizing their plans. Getting others involved at critical junctures to provide input and feedback is different from delegating the task to others. It maintains responsibility at the top while demonstrating respect for the ideas and knowledge of others.

Improvement Strategy, Step 3: Awareness

The awareness phase is where everything that has been done in the first two steps is communicated to the organization. For the first time, the entire organization is formally introduced to the philosophy, direction, and approach developed by the steering council. Phase 2 training is undertaken to gain people's understanding and commitment. Top management must make an effort to reassure people that the quality initiative is serious and not just another fad. This is the opportunity to capture the hearts and minds of the people, to have them adopt the improvement vision as their own and believe that the pursuit of quality plays a key role in their collective well-being. Taking this step means committing to a strategy of continuous improvement, which is a never-ending pursuit. Top management puts its credibility on the line. Once the awareness step is begun, there is no turning back.

Communicate the Quality Imperative

Strategies, visions, goals, quality management systems, and plans are not much use unless people know about them. What is needed is a multifaceted communications approach to let everyone know on an ongoing basis that quality is a priority and progress is being made. Unfortunately, communication is the least understood and most poorly managed aspect of many total quality management implementations. People form their opinions about management's dedication to quality not only by what is said, but also by watching what happens every day in the workplace. They watch what top managers do to see what the priorities really are. Executives must be ever-mindful that everything they say and do will be scrutinized for consistency with their publicly avowed commitment to improvement.

A recent study of quality leadership found that effective leaders believe their primary task is to promote the vision of customer-focused quality throughout the organization, and they use all available forms of communication to do this (Brager, 1992). Frederick Smith of Federal Express feels that "creating trust through open, candid communications is at the heart of the effort. I am not sure how a service company can survive without candid, two-way communications, which we consider absolutely essential to achieving our goals" (Smith, 1990).

Speeches are a personal way for executives to communicate their commitment publicly and let people know what they think is important. Videotaping is the next-best option to communicate with people who cannot be reached personally and those who join the organization later. A regular place in the company newsletter should be dedicated to articles about quality progress. The periodic employee or management meetings that companies normally conduct need to incorporate the quality theme. Executive memoranda, quarterly earnings statements, and annual reports provide opportunities to reinforce the quality message. Staff meetings and operations reviews should be used as daily reminders that quality is as important as costs and schedules.

Conduct Phase 2 Training
(Gaining Understanding and Commitment)

Phase 2 training is the initial quality indoctrination for the entire organization. The overall objectives of this phase are to help people understand the company's direction and leave them feeling personally committed to participating in the improvement process. This phase of training articulates management's philosophy of improvement, its vision and plan for the company, and the philosophy and fundamentals of quality. Training can help people understand what quality means to them at work every day and stress to them that improvement is a primary expectation and job requirement of everyone. Phase 2 training also gives people an overview of the quality tools, techniques, and methodology that will be covered in depth in subsequent phases of training. It helps them see that improvement means people working cooperatively to identify, solve, and prevent problems. Finally, Phase 2 training is a call to begin the process.

Improvement Strategy, Step 4: Deployment

This fourth step addresses the difficult question of how to deploy the improvement strategy throughout the organization and into the company's supplier base. Once people get the quality message and understand the basics, they need a system and an infrastructure to focus and support their efforts. The improvement team infrastructure is the engine that powers the process and turns a paper strategy into reality. Deployment involves five related activities: conducting Phase 3 quality systems training, organizing an improvement team infrastructure, conducting Phase 4 training for teams, holding individuals responsible for improvement, and driving improvement into the supplier base.

Conduct Phase 3 Training
(Building a Quality Management System)

The third phase of training lets everyone understand how all facets of the improvement process fit together. People need to understand how the quality management system coordinates their efforts. If the organization's objective is to get certified as an ISO 9000 supplier or to apply for the Baldrige Award, everyone must know what needs to happen and what individual responsibilities are. A small cadre of experienced people must also be trained as assessors to help put the QMS in place. The members of this group become the internal experts on the QMS; they train others, provide consulting support, and audit the operations in relation to the criteria. The extent of the training people need in this area depends on the complexity of the system that the organization adopts or develops.

Organize an Improvement Team Infrastructure

Sustained improvement requires more than excellent individual performance. It requires the coordinated effort of people throughout the organization, working in teams. The foundation of the improvement team infrastructure is the corporate steering council. The steering council directs the overall improvement effort by deciding on the corporate philosophy, quality management system, broad goals and plans, and system of accountability. The next level of management then organizes itself to drive improvement through all divisions or departments in the company. Improvement councils within each division provide the local leadership needed to translate broad corporate goals into meaningful operational objectives and to facilitate implementation. Division councils are made up of the division vice president or general manager and the immediate staff representing all major functional areas and departments. In addition to providing leadership and direction, the major responsibilities of the division councils are to remove obstacles in the paths of improvement teams and facilitate interdepartmental cooperation.

The division improvement councils establish a variety of improvement teams throughout the organization. Teams normally include "intact," or departmental, teams and "cross-functional," or interdepartmental, teams. Departmental teams are set up to improve the work processes they independently control. Interdepartmental teams are set up to improve business processes that cut across departments or functions, such as new-product introductions and accounts payable processing. These areas offer significant opportunities for improvement, but they can be addressed only through cooperation and teamwork across traditional departmental boundaries. The number and types of teams a division establishes will depend on the nature of its goals and the extent to which teamwork is a normal part of the environment. Organizations with little history of team-based activity are advised to limit the number of teams they initially set up. People need a chance to get used to group work and to experience some early successes that can be used as models for others to follow.

A distinction needs to be drawn between "quality circles" and these improvement teams. Quality circles have been effectively used in Japan for many years, but they were introduced in the United States in the early 1970s with only limited success. Masaaki Imai (1986) defines a quality circle as "a small group that voluntarily performs quality-control activities within the shop. The small group carries out its work continuously as part of a company-wide program of quality control, self-development, mutual education, and flow control and improvement within the workshop. The quality control circle is only part of a company-wide program; it is never the whole of total quality control or company-wide quality control" (p. 11). In the United

States, quality circles have been used to increase employee involvement, but too frequently, such efforts were not anchored in a broad-based improvement strategy. Operating by themselves, they often failed to achieve significant, ongoing results.

By contrast, improvement teams are groups specifically formed to pursue the goals developed by the corporate and division improvement councils. Rather than being voluntary, as in the classical quality circle approach, participation in improvement teams is considered a basic job responsibility. Working in improvement teams is not seen as an activity conducted outside of normal work processes but rather as part of the way the company does business. Fortunately, the basic skills and training needed for quality circles and improvement teams are similar. Making the transition from isolated quality circles to an improvement team structure tied to the company's quality strategy is necessary and not particularly difficult.

Conduct Phase 4 Training (Empowering Improvement Teams)

The training provided to improvement teams consists of teaching the skills people need to effectively solve problems in groups. They include meeting management, problem solving, and decision making, in addition to the use of basic quality tools such as brainstorming, checksheets, histograms, Pareto diagrams, cause and effect diagrams, scatter diagrams, and other graphs. Statistical process control, which is frequently taught in conjunction with these simple tools, is addressed separately in the next phase of training. People need to master the basic group process skills first and learn how to work together in teams before they try to tackle the more complex statistical techniques.

Team training is most effective when it is conducted immediately before the requirement to use the skills or in conjunction with the actual performance of a task. Delays between the time people are trained and their first opportunities to apply the skills result in a loss of learning and should be avoided.

Hold Individuals Responsible for Improvement

Although it is true that team efforts are required to address the significant issues organizations face and to achieve the "critical mass" needed to sustain improvement, it is also true that people have the responsibility to vigorously pursue improvements in their individual jobs. That responsibility includes everything from gaining a better understanding of what internal customers require to controlling and improving individual work processes. Everyone has dual responsibilities: first, to participate in improvement team activities; and second, to integrate the quality philosophy and tools into everything they do. The quality vision and strategy come alive when individuals can translate organizational goals into their day-to-day activities.

With responsibility comes accountability, and it is up to managers to build quality into their expectations of people as well as into their individual goal setting and performance appraisal processes. If Michael LeBoeuf (1985, p. 23) is right, and "the things that get rewarded get done," then we had better make sure that people are held accountable for improvement and that their efforts are recognized and rewarded.

Form Supplier Partnerships

Most organizations are not self-sufficient; they depend on suppliers for a variety of goods and services. The quality of these goods and services can have a major impact on a company's ability to satisfy its customers' needs. Therefore, the complete system of quality interdependencies extends from a company's suppliers (and their suppliers) through all of its own internal processes and, ultimately, to the end user or consumer. Companies that make progress in reducing their costs and improving their quality and cycle times are the ones that strive to form partnerships with suppliers and integrate them into their overall improvement strategy. Such partnerships require extensive communication and resource sharing.

Communicating a company's commitment to quality

throughout its supplier base can take many forms, from the fine print of the purchase order or volume purchase agreement to training for the supplier's employees. The World Class Supplier Program, developed by Compaq Computer Corporation, is an example of an excellent supplier communication program. In May 1990, Compaq executives organized a conference for their key suppliers around the world. The speakers at the conference were the company's top executives in quality, materials, purchasing, engineering, and manufacturing. Participants received a comprehensive notebook, titled *World Class Supplier Process: Framework for Material Improvement* (Compaq Computer Corporation, 1990). In addition to background information about Compaq and its supplier partnership philosophy, the notebook contains the following seven sections: quality improvement for business partners, supplier quality survey, process capability and evaluation, measurement system analysis and evaluation, scatter diagrams and correlation analysis, product evaluation, and supplier-generated change requests. The World Class Supplier Program very effectively communicates what Compaq expects from its suppliers in terms of quality—from its philosophy of business partnerships to its standards for supplier control of measurement equipment and manufacturing processes.

Training is often an important form of communication and resource sharing. The most comprehensive supplier training is undoubtedly provided through the Motorola Supplier Institute. The six-day institute is composed of the following courses: Understanding Six Sigma (one day); Manufacturing Cycle Reduction (two days); Design for Manufacturability (two days); and Practical Implementation Strategies for Design of Experiments (one day). Motorola also encourages participation in any of the other courses listed in its catalogue, which is titled *Supplier/Customer Training: A Proven Partnership in Quality* (Motorola University, 1990). These courses range from customer satisfaction and statistical process control to benchmarking and the development of quality software. Programs like Compaq's and Motorola's exemplify what can be done to help a company's suppliers understand what to do and how to do it.

Improvement Strategy, Step 5: Implementation

The fifth step of the improvement strategy is where improvement actually takes place. The four preceding steps set the stage for implementing improvement, which includes defining, controlling, and improving work processes. Implementation also involves Phase 5 training.

Conduct Phase 5 Training
(Improving Production and Business Processes)

Once improvement teams are functioning well and are able to collect, display, and analyze data, they need to learn one or both of the following: statistical process control and business process improvement. Both require a thorough understanding of the concepts of prevention, variation, process capability, and structured methodology. The use of these techniques is the first major step away from "fighting fires" and containing problems toward reducing variation and preventing problems.

Statistical process control uses control charts to identify special causes of variation in important processes. Once they are identified, they can be investigated, and appropriate corrective action can then be taken.

The focus of business process improvement is cutting across organizational boundaries to eliminate unnecessary bureaucracy, no-value-added steps, and duplication. According to the 1991 Baldrige Award guidelines, "business processes and support activities might include activities and operations involving finance and accounting, software services, sales, marketing, information services, purchasing, personnel, legal services, plant and facilities management, research and development, and secretarial and administrative services" (National Institute of Standards and Technology, 1990, p. 14). A variety of tools are used to make business processes more effective, efficient, and foolproof in the interest of reducing costs and serving customers better. Process control and improvement are the very heart of the whole quality effort.

Improve Work Processes

Phase 5 training enables improvement teams to define, analyze, control, and improve the work processes that have a major impact on the quality of a company's products and services. Guided by the corporate and division improvement objectives, teams can proceed with the difficult task of figuring out how to continuously improve both manufacturing and business processes.

This is the step where management's commitment is tested. Will people be supported when they want to initiate change? What decision will be made when an improvement effort appears to conflict with the accomplishment of short-term objectives? Will management's initial enthusiasm for improvement begin to wane as the work load of continuous improvement looms larger? Will people continue to be given time to participate in improvement team activities when the crush of other responsibilities mounts? The ways managers at all levels respond to these questions over time will determine whether improvement can really be an effective strategy for an organization.

Improvement Strategy, Step 6: Continuous Improvement

The most difficult lesson to learn when pursuing quality is that improvement is an ongoing, never-ending process. Bill Almon, president of Conner Peripherals, has likened the American improvement ethic and international competition to our fascination with football:

> We want to think about global competition as if it were the Superbowl. We want to play hard for the season, win the big game, and sit around during the off-season and gloat about how great we are. But the competition we face in business today doesn't want to wait until next year for a rematch—

they want to play again next week and every week until they finally win. It's tough for us to accept that we don't control the rules of the game any-more. We've got to be ready to battle tough com-petitors every day, forever, without a break.

This sense of urgency must be permanently instilled in everyone in the organization. To ensure that improvement is a closed-loop, never-ending process, the organization must com-mit to assessing and rewarding progress, resetting improve-ment goals, and implementing Phase 6 training.

Assess and Reward Progress

Progress is only possible with accountability, and accountability comes from management taking time to assess the organization's progress toward its improvement goals. People have the uncanny ability to discern the difference between management's stated and real goals. Stated goals are what we say we want to do; real goals are what we really care about and spend our precious time on. Too frequently, costs, schedules, volume, revenue, and margins are emphasized in business review meetings, while quality is seldom mentioned. Effectively following up on goals, plans, and progress is as important to sustaining improvement over time as the improvement activi-ties themselves. Ensuring that management's stated quality goals are aligned with its real business goals means regularly following up with people about their progress and managing quality as other key indicators of corporate performance are managed.

Understanding why people are or are not "doing quality" requires looking more closely at the behaviors and results the organization actually rewards. What happens to people who believe in the stated goal of quality and come into conflict with a goal like meeting the schedule? Are they supported or coun-termanded? Are they rewarded or punished? When bonuses are handed out or the next person is promoted into manage-ment, are accomplishments in quality a deciding factor? When people's performance appraisals are written at the end of the year or the next story is written for the company newsletter, is improvement highlighted and praised? The answers to these questions determine the extent to which people will believe in the organization's stated quality goals and feel empowered to take action. According to John Akers, CEO of IBM, "you empower people by education, by example, and by any other way you can think of, including making heroes of people who have taken the initiative and done something without always checking with their managers" (Bemowski, 1991).

Reset Improvement Goals

Continuous improvement means constantly setting challenging goals, meeting them, and setting ever-higher goals. It means controlling work processes, reducing sources of variation, controlling processes at new levels of performance, and finding ways to reduce variation further. One of the major accomplishments of IBM's Market Driven Quality effort, says Akers, has been to change people's "mind-set from 'incremental improvement is the goal' to 'incremental improvement is all right, but perfection is required.' That is a huge, huge difference in mind-set" (Bemowski, 1991). He goes on to say that we must go beyond just meeting customer requirements to getting everybody in the company "to think in terms of delighting his or her customer." The 1990–1995 strategic plan for the IBM Rochester facility, the site that won the 1990 Baldrige Award, calls for reducing its cycle time by an additional 50 percent and reaching a consistent six-sigma level of product defects from its estimated current level of three to six sigma.

John Galvin set increasingly challenging improvement goals for Motorola throughout the decade of the 1980s. Motorola's goal in the early 1980s was a tenfold increase in measured quality in five years. After largely achieving that goal, Galvin challenged his company again in a company-wide message in January 1987 to improve product and service quality ten times by 1989 and to achieve six-sigma capability by 1992 (Gill, 1990). Setting demanding yet achievable goals paid off for Motorola: a twenty-seven-person unit in the main manufacturing plant celebrated its 255th straight week without a defect in late 1989.

Meeting initial improvement goals is a significant accomplishment and should be celebrated. But we cannot afford to become complacent about our accomplishments and get caught sitting around during the off-season and gloating about how great we are. We must continually ask ourselves challenging questions: What are our competitors doing to move ahead of us in the marketplace? What will our customers be expecting from us next? What can we do to "delight" them with our products and services?

As David Kearns reminds us, "it's tough work and we will never get there because quality improvement is an ongoing process. We must continually reset our expectation levels—expectation levels that, today, are above anything that people even thought about two or three years ago. Two or three years from now we will have to reset them again" (Kearns, 1988).

Implement Phase 6 Training (Creating a Learning Organization)

Training, like the improvement process itself, must be a continuous, ongoing activity. People's knowledge, skills, and abilities must keep pace with technological and market-driven developments. The quality training curriculum is not a static, fixed path that people march down to completion. Continuous improvement requires continuous learning of new and innovative ways to stay a step ahead of the competition and satisfy customers' expectations.

Tom Peters insists that "life-long learning *is* the organization. That is, we are going to have to *describe our companies* in terms of the skill pool we have, relative to the competition. . . . The ultimate question for management is: Is the skill pool of my work force, relative to the needs of the future, getting better faster than my competitors' is?" (Gordon, 1989). The next training challenge is transforming improvement from a series of isolated events into a process of ongoing learning that facilitates the evolution of quality in organizations.

The first five phases of training provide people with the

basic skills they need to get the improvement process under way. Although training in more advanced methods can be done at any time they are required, it is most effective after the basics of improvement are firmly established. Advanced management methods include the use of such techniques as Hoshin planning, the seven new quality tools, and quality function deployment. An example of advanced quantitative methods would be Taguchi techniques. The choice of which methods to use depends on the requirements of the business and the readiness of the individuals involved.

Companies also conduct a variety of other training in addition to the strictly quality-oriented training that is the subject of this book. Such training normally includes management and supervisory development, product and technology training, and sales training. All should be seen as supporting the overall improvement effort. The skills of delegating, setting goals, and giving performance feedback, which have long been taught in management classes, attain greater significance and impact when applied in the context of leading the improvement process. The same is true of the skills taught in basic sales training, such as developing rapport and trust, soliciting needs, negotiating, and resolving conflict. The traditional walls between training specialties should be broken down and their combined efforts focused toward the common goal of improvement.

Two Caveats

It is important to state two caveats at this point, one about the improvement process in general and one about training for quality in particular. First, anyone who has been involved in an effort to improve quality knows it is a messy business. The process is always plagued by strong personalities, organizational politics, conflicting priorities, skepticism, confusion, and false starts. No matter how hard you try, improvement is never easy and never goes smoothly. If taken at face value, the six-step improvement strategy presented here is an unrealistic picture of what you will experience as you proceed down the path of improvement. It is virtually guaranteed that, sooner or later, you will want to throw up your hands and wish you had never heard the cursed word *quality*. The level of frustration is bound to go higher before it goes lower. The six-step strategy and six-phase training curriculum do not magically lead to quality.

Senge (1990b) reminds us that "strategy is less a rational plan arrived at in the abstract and implemented throughout the organization than an 'emergent phenomenon.' Successful organizations craft strategy . . . as they continually learn about shifting business conditions and balance what is desired and what is possible. The key is not getting the right strategy but fostering strategic thinking." The improvement strategy presented here is intended to help you navigate around the many unexpected obstacles. Although the six steps and various substeps will not happen in a neat and orderly way, they provide a general framework whose essential components and basic sequence should be considered whenever the decision is made to take an alternative path. Sequence and timing have a lot to do with success.

The second caveat has to do with the limitations of training. This first chapter may give the impression that the real obstacle to improvement is lack of knowledge—a problem that training presumably helps solve. Although this is true to a certain extent, most people innately know much more about quality than they put into practice on a daily basis. Then why do people not do what they already know should be done? In part, they lack the knowledge and applied skills that training can provide. In part, the inertia of the "system" somehow keeps them from doing the right things. The problem may even be myopic top managers who are hounded by Wall Street to focus on short-term results.

But the main difficulty we have in pursuing quality has much to do with the way we think about the world of work in general. In many ways we go about work much as primitive human beings went about finding shelter or obtaining food to survive. When our predecessors were cold or hungry, the only objective was to satisfy the need, presumably with little concern about the process that was used. We continue to pride ourselves on our instrumental approach to the world, thinking of it as hard-nosed business acumen, with such familiar statements as "I only want to hear about the results, not how you get them." We are conditioned to value highly the attainment of the objective and to value little the means or process used to achieve it. The result is valued, the process is not.

However, improvement is a process, and quality is the result. Quality cannot be improved directly; it is the result of improving the process used to produce the product or service. Since we do not value the process per se, we find it difficult to justify even to ourselves—let alone our bosses—the time, effort, and investment that are required to improve it. And there's the rub. We value and desire the result, quality or customer satisfaction, but not the means to obtain it. We have neither the patience nor the faith required to improve the process with the hope that sometime in the future we will get the results we desire. We want to go directly to the result, which, unfortunately for us, is not possible when pursuing quality. Under this type of results-at-any-cost management, as Senge (1990b) notes, "an organization hurtles from crisis to crisis. Eventually, the worldview of people in the organization becomes dominated by events and reactiveness. Many, especially those who are deeply committed, become burned out. Eventually cynicism comes to pervade the organization. People have no control over their time, let alone their destiny."

A manifestation of the process-results dilemma is the unstated assumption that it is possible to have happy customers without first having happy employees. There is a prevalent belief that we can have two different standards of behavior— one we exhibit externally with our customers and one we exhibit internally with ourselves. Once again, we want to obtain the result we desire, happy customers, without first addressing the process, which is modeling customer-oriented behavior within our organizations and improving employee morale. A sample of comments from executives who have achieved significant improvement should lead us to abandon this self-deception quickly:

- *Robert Paluck, of Convex Computers:* "The whole driving force behind this (maintaining a positive corporate culture) is that you don't believe you can have happy customers unless you have intensely happy employees. You can't have one without the other" (Baatz, 1991).
- *Charles Crawley, president of Maryland Bank:* "Create an environment that makes people feel good and supports their enthusiastic pursuit of customer satisfaction. . . . When people feel good, they transmit that feeling to their job. They satisfy the customer" (Stratton, 1990a).
- *Fredrick W. Smith, chair and CEO of Federal Express:* "I believe that customer dedication mirrors the extent to which an organization demonstrates commitment to its employees. . . . In our search for the human side of quality, we learned a long time ago that employee satisfaction is a prerequisite to customer satisfaction. . . . We believe that, when our people are placed first, they will provide the highest possible service, and profits will follow" (1990).

As Peter Block points out in *The Empowered Manager,* "you can't treat your customers any better than you treat each other. . . . We have to manage our people in a way that is absolutely aligned with the way we want our customers and users to be managed. We can't use fear and punishment to improve customer service. Our employees' ultimate revenge is to take out on our customers resentment and frustration that should rightly be aimed at us" (1991, p. 119).

There are no shortcuts to quality and customer satisfaction. We must believe that creating a positive environment within our organizations will promote customer-oriented behavior by employees. Our attitudes are deeply rooted in our results-only mind-set. A "paradigm shift" is required to enable us to move to a fix-the-process-to-improve-the-results way of thinking. Training is undoubtedly our best available lever to help us make that shift, as long as we understand we are struggling against a cultural predisposition and are persistent in our efforts.

2

Building a
Leadership Foundation

THE RESPONSIBILITY FOR
quality starts at the top of the organization. "An obstacle to
participation by upper management," however, says quality
guru Joseph Juran, "is their limited experience and training in
managing for quality. They have extensive experience in management of business and finance but not in managing quality"
(1986). Phase 1 of the training process therefore starts with
none other than top management.

Dilemmas in Training Executives

This simple concept, that quality and quality training must start
in the executive suite, has been one of the most elusive in the
entire quest for improvement. This elusiveness results from
several key problems peculiar to training high-level managers.
Those hoping to establish viable improvement processes in
their organizations must successfully address these daunting
dilemmas: resistance to training, lack of understanding, inappropriate delegation, hope for "instant pudding," and lack of
staff credibility.

This chapter strives to define the nature of these dilemmas and describe how to organize the executive training process and curriculum to successfully overcome them. At a broader

level, it outlines a methodology to help executives complete the first two steps of the improvement strategy and build a strong leadership foundation for the entire improvement process.

Resistance to Training

Executives are successful people, having attained the highest levels of position, power, money, and influence available in organizational life. They would not be where they are if they were not smart and capable. These obvious facts are undeniable. What is less obvious to people of power and authority is the need to continuously learn and expand their perspectives.

Albert Einstein once observed that the significant problems we face cannot be solved at the same level of thinking we were at when we created them. This simple quote has two important implications for executives. The first is accepting that their current thinking and past actions have resulted in the quality problems they now face. The second implication is the need to change their thinking if they want different results. The most formidable barriers to improvement may well be top managers' reluctance to admit their own culpability in today's problems and their need to educate themselves about quality.

Lack of Understanding

The reluctance to accept their own role leads many executives to believe they understand the improvement process when they really do not and to rely on what Philip Crosby calls "conventional wisdom":

> The first struggle, and it is never over, is to overcome the "conventional wisdom" regarding quality. In some mysterious way each new manager becomes imbued with this conventional wisdom. It says that quality is goodness; that it is unmeasurable; and that people just don't give a damn about doing good work. No matter what company they work for, or where they went to school, or where they were raised—they all believe

> something erroneous like this. But in real life,
> quality is something quite different. . . . Error is
> not required to fulfill the laws of nature; and
> people work just as hard now as they ever did. . . .
> What should be obvious from the outset is that
> people perform to the standards of their leaders
> [Crosby, 1979, pp. 7–8].

Helping executives see that they really do not understand when they think they do can be taken as a challenge to authority. It is a delicate process to be handled with great care even by other top managers, let alone subordinate staff members.

Inappropriate Delegation

Lack of understanding is both a cause and an effect of the tendency to delegate the development of quality strategy and policy to those far removed from the levels normally involved in other strategic issues. Executives often believe they can delegate "quality" to others in the same way they delegate routine business tasks. The performance of specific quality-related tasks can certainly be delegated, but active quality leadership cannot.

On the other hand, inappropriate delegation can reinforce executive lack of understanding. As Ross Gilbert of Kohler Company points out, "delegation of planning means delegation of understanding. Planning requires research and analysis. The level of understanding that comes from this effort cannot be transmitted completely in a report or presentation. It is available only through direct involvement in the assessment phase of program development" (1990). There is no substitute for direct, personal involvement to strengthen both understanding and leadership.

"Hope for Instant Pudding"

Deming (1982) calls the "hope for instant pudding" one of the chief obstacles to improvement: "An important obstacle is the supposition that improvement of quality and productivity is accomplished suddenly by an affirmation of faith" (p. 126). This supposition can take any of several forms: hiring an expensive consultant to chide management and show them the way, going en masse to seminars conducted by one or more of the gurus, or conducting an internal publicity campaign that extols quality and exhorts workers to try harder to satisfy the customer. ·

The difficult truth, though, is that improvement is a long-term process that requires extensive training and a lot of hard work. Bottom-line results seldom appear suddenly to save a troubled customer account or a poor financial quarter. Quality consultant David Nadler quoted the CEO of a major corporate client as saying, "The more I get into this quality thing, the more I realize two things: First, it is really tough. In fact, if I had known how hard this would be when we first started, I might not have chosen to do it! Second, I'm now even more convinced that we have to do quality. It's critical that we do it, and ultimately we have no choice" (Cornell and Herman, 1989). Patience and long-term commitment, uncommon traits in business, are still virtues when it comes to improvement.

Lack of Staff Credibility

Although no outside consulting group can provide an instant cure for an organization's quality problems, hiring one is necessary when it comes to training top managers. A lesson familiar to many internal training and quality departments is corroborated by the experience of quality guru Joseph Juran: "Upper managers are reluctant to accept insiders or subordinates as instructors" (1989, p. 332). This is a difficult fact of organizational life, which internal quality experts, advocates, and trainers have to accept. As a particularly blunt executive once commented to a change-oriented staff member, "If you're so smart, why aren't you running the company instead of me?" It is tough to be a prophet in your own land, especially in the early stages of quality. Staff time is more productively spent in identifying an effective, compatible consultant than in struggling for recognition and credibility early in the training of top managers.

Organizing Executive Training

Phase 1 training for executives must be organized properly in order to avoid or resolve these dilemmas. Although the content of executive training is in many ways similar to that provided to others in Phase 2, the way it is organized and delivered is much different. The five activities involved in organizing executive training are selecting the right consultant, getting executives off-site, making objectives tangible, establishing a results-driven format, and getting the right speakers.

Selecting the Right Consultant

Selecting the right consultant helps overcome the internal credibility problem and can be pivotal in getting off to a good start. Take care to pick the person who is right for the organization; don't just look for credentials. A common problem with the larger consulting groups is that the person who makes the sale is often different from the one who actually does the consulting work. Personal rapport is crucial, especially in this first phase. Beware of signing up with the principal of a consulting firm who will subsequently delegate the work to staffers.

The most important thing in selecting the right consultant is to know what you want. What do you really want the consultant to do? What type of relationship do you want? Some consultants focus on the strategic end of quality, and many are capable of tactical implementation. The consultant who has the strategic capability needed on the front end of the process may not be the same consultant you will need later for assisting with such tactical issues as work force training. Assuming you know what you want, consider the following consultant characteristics when making the selection:

- Experience in guiding successful improvement efforts of diverse organizations or industries
- Ability to establish rapport quickly with the different personalities of the management team

- Knowledge of the various quality models, tools, and techniques
- Ability to quickly perceive the underlying issues in the organization
- Flexibility and willingness to adapt the consultant's approach to the unique needs of the organization, rather than imposing a canned solution
- Ability to help the client become independent of the consultant while also wanting to maintain a long-term, mutually beneficial relationship
- High satisfaction ratings from previous clients
- Direct experience working with top managers and, most importantly, the willingness to tell them the truth

Getting Executives Off-Site

One way to ensure the failure of initial efforts to train top managers is to conduct their training on company premises, within earshot of every hiccup and false start in the business. Given their preference for being in the middle of the action, coupled with a strong resistance to training, executives will take advantage of any opportunity to escape the training process by responding to operational issues.

The only hope for gaining executives' attention for an appreciable period of time is to get them away from the office. Conduct the initial executive session as an executive retreat. It should be far enough from the office to make returning home impractical and close enough not to waste people's time traveling. Resist the natural executive desire to push for an unrealistically brief schedule, and plan enough time for participants to immerse themselves in the subject and get something done. Two to three days is usually sufficient to meet the objectives; more than three days will normally meet with resistance.

Making Objectives Tangible

Results-driven executives need to have the session objectives stated in clear, task-oriented terms. The objectives of this first phase of training are as clear and tangible as they are challenging: to complete the first two steps of the improvement strategy.

Although considerable learning will be involved, the instructional aspects of the experience should be de-emphasized.

Completing these steps, which begin to establish the necessary leadership foundation, is clearly a lot of work—more work than can possibly be accomplished in a single, off-site meeting. The initial retreat is just a beginning. The preparation and planning steps will likely take four sessions or more to complete, over a period as long as three to six months. Taking less than three months is probably unrealistic, and people's initial enthusiasm will begin to fade rapidly if the process drags beyond six months. There are few shortcuts or ways to circumvent what needs to be done.

The tendency of top managers to demand quick results goes hand in hand with the habit and need to delegate tasks to others. Once a task has been delegated, it is natural to become impatient with another's performance. When top managers are directly involved and are faced with the realization of how much work they themselves must do and how long it takes, however, the hope for "instant pudding" quickly fades into a more sober appreciation for the long-term nature of improvement.

Establishing a Results-Driven Format

Executive training should be structured to achieve an ongoing series of tangible outcomes in order to meet executives' expectations and achieve their objectives. The most effective format for this is a three-part "learn-apply-do" learning cycle. New concepts or information should be presented so participants can then reflect on it and apply it to their own situation. After understanding a concept in general and how to apply it under specific circumstances, participants should then use it to complete a task or create an outcome.

An example of the learn-apply-do learning method is the creation of a quality vision. Executives must first understand what a vision is and why it is important to guiding the entire improvement process (learn). They need to think about how the concept of a quality vision relates to existing company values and other stated or unstated cultural norms (apply) and then create such a vision for the company (do). This format allows participants to learn from their experience in the process of accomplishing tangible objectives. According to Texaco's head of executive development, Robert Mann, "experiential learning—learning by doing—will receive significantly more emphasis as a learning method in executive education programs in the future. Formal executive education will include action learning. In other words, it will offer a forum in which teams learn by working to resolve real business issues" (Mann and Staudenmier, 1991).

Getting the Right Speakers

In addition to having an experienced consultant lead the training sessions, other outside speakers can be brought in on selected subjects to help overcome the internal credibility problem. As Juran advises, executives "are eager listeners to the experience of upper managers from well-managed companies, especially the chief executive officers of such companies, . . . [and] are willing to visit companies that have earned recognition through their quality" (1989, p. 332). Testimony from other top managers speaks much louder than standard training presentations. Stories of victories and defeats, what worked and what did not, and how they continued in the face of adversity and skepticism help move executives from intellectual acknowledgment to gut-level belief in quality.

Getting such speakers for the training is easier than it may seem. People like to share their experiences with interested colleagues and feel complimented when asked to do so. Sources can include customer companies, suppliers, and executive or industry contacts. And all winners of the Malcolm Baldrige National Quality Award are "expected to share information about their successful quality strategies with other U.S. organizations" (National Institute of Standards and Technology, 1990, p. 1).

Executive Curriculum

Understanding executive training dilemmas and how to organize training to avoid them is an important beginning. Next comes the task of structuring the curriculum. The stated objective of this first phase of training is to have executives learn about and complete the first two steps of the improvement strategy: preparation and planning. The broader, unstated objectives are to obtain top management's understanding and agreement on what quality means to the business and to get their commitment to constancy of purpose in pursuing improvement. Starting a quality "program" is easy to do. Sticking with it and weaving improvement into the fabric of the organization is not. Deming calls "lack of constancy of purpose" the "crippling disease" of quality efforts (p. 98).

The assumption underlying the instructional design presented here is that people, especially top managers, learn best when they learn from guided experience relative to things they care about. Talking about quality in theory achieves little beyond intellectual awareness and assent. People need to become immersed in quality indirectly by working on the issues they already understand to be critical to their success—such as what their customers think, what the competition is doing, and what their costs are. They will develop their own appreciation of the importance of quality and in the process become personally committed to its realization. In completing the preparation and planning steps of the strategy, senior managers become more knowledgeable about quality and more committed to the constant purpose of improvement.

The content, objectives, and general process for training are clear. What cannot be predicted with as much precision is how best to package the learning experiences or how long it will take to meet the needs of every group. The four-session structure shown in Figure 2.1 is an effective framework for executive training, but it should be treated flexibly and adapted to each organization. Presenting the curriculum as a series of four results-driven sessions of limited duration is usually acceptable to most top managers. The likelihood is that more than four meetings may be required, in which case it is better to have executives come to that conclusion on their own.

Session 1: Assessing the Quality Position and Developing a Shared Vision

Again, the overall objective of the first session is to develop creative tension, the discomfort an individual feels when confronted with a difference between the current state (where we

Figure 2.1. Phase 1 Training: Building a Leadership Foundation.

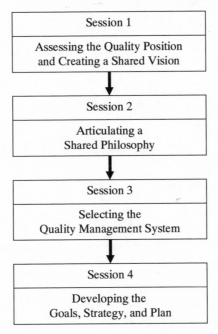

are) and the desired state (where we would like to be). This discomfort provides the motivation needed to overcome the discrepancy between the two, and this motivation is the seed that will later bloom into the full-blown executive commitment that is required. Therefore, the first session involves the four main activities shown in Figure 2.2.

Prework for the Session

Hold an organizing meeting with participants before the first session to clarify expectations and help them get prepared. Ask the heads of sales, marketing, quality, and human resources to bring information on customer feedback, competitive position, costs of nonconformance, and employee satisfaction, respectively. Let them know they will be expected to make presentations on their findings at the first session and lead discussions on the implications.

Also prior to the session, try to stimulate the thinking of all participants about the importance of quality to the organi-

**Figure 2.2. Session 1: Assessing the Quality Position
and Creating a Shared Vision.**

zation, perhaps by distributing relevant, thought-provoking articles or reports and asking participants to be prepared to discuss them. One such report is *U.S. Companies Improve Performance Through Quality Efforts* (1991), published by the U.S. General Accounting Office. This report clearly demonstrates that, "in nearly all cases, companies that used quality management practices achieved better employee relations, higher productivity, greater customer satisfaction, increased market share, and improved profitability" (p. 2).

Another stimulating reading is an earlier study of over six hundred businesses in diverse industries, published in the *Journal of Marketing*. Phillips, Chang, and Buzzell (1983) go beyond showing the correlation between quality and other business measures to demonstrate that superior quality is the *causal* factor in superior financial and market performance. Correlations between quality and profitability have even been demonstrated in health care. A study of hospitals showed that "providing quality care for cancer surgery had a $276 contribution to margin per Medicare discharge. The lowest quality group lost $1,100 per Medicare discharge" (Everett and James, 1991). These are the types of findings that can influence how top managers think about quality even before they come to the first training session.

Understanding Quality's Impact on the Business

The objective of this exercise is to help executives realize that improvement is the best strategy for achieving their bottom-line business objectives. The discussion can be started by reviewing the findings of the study assigned as part of the session prework. Use the Total Quality Management Model described in the General Accounting Office report to quickly stimulate a lively discussion among participants. Try to uncover any disagreements with the relationships shown in the model between product and service quality and other business measures. Ask individuals direct questions about whether their experience supports or conflicts with the model.

Have executives discuss the relationship of improved quality to issues like customer satisfaction, financial performance, operating procedures, and employee relations. The purpose is to get them thinking about the applicability of these reported relationships to the company. Do they think these same relationships exist within their organizations? If not, why not? If so, what are the implications for their priorities and how priorities are set in the organization? Talking about the impact of quality on the bottom-line measures they already care about helps drive home the importance of focusing on improvement as a business strategy.

Assessing the Quality Position

Assessment of the organization's quality position requires examining four sources of information: customer feedback, competitive analysis, costs of nonconformance, and employee satisfaction. Each source of information provides a different perspective and leads to a better understanding of where the organization stands and where improvement is needed.

Customer Feedback. The first part of the assessment must come from customers, since customers define quality. Their buying preferences are determined by how satisfied they are with a company's products and services. Bert Staniar, chairman of Westinghouse Broadcast Company, puts the mentality of today's customer in harsh perspective: "Today's customer is smarter, tougher, and less forgiving than ever before. Today, the customer comes prewired to be cynical, disloyal, and just plain ornery. He has been taught to demand quality, service, and greatness. He hears the words over and over again everywhere, and he's come to see it as his birthright" (Harrington, 1991, p. ix). To attract and keep today's discerning and disloyal customers, companies need regular and accurate feedback from them about their likes and dislikes.

Of all inputs to the strategic planning process noted in Ernst & Young (1992), the most dramatic change "is the increase in the importance of customer satisfaction measures. Three years from now [in 1995], 70 percent of companies expect that customer satisfaction measures will be of 'primary' importance in the strategic planning process," compared to only 34 percent currently and 19 percent three years ago (p. 43). This expectation, however, stands in contradiction to the failure of North American companies to recognize the value of customer complaint systems as a primary source of information for the identification of new products and services: "Three years from now, companies in the United States and Canada will be using customer complaint information at only the levels companies in Japan and Germany used three years ago"—approximately 41 to 44 percent (p. 29). Currently, 72 percent of German and 60 percent of Japanese companies use complaint information for this purpose, and they plan to increase over three years to 80 percent (p. 29). All sources of customer feedback and input should be used in the quality assessment and planning process.

The head of sales or customer service should present the customer satisfaction data and objectively point up the organization's perceived strengths and weaknesses. Sources can include customer satisfaction surveys, complaint logs, interviews, focus groups, customer letters, and analyses of recent customer gains and losses. Discussing these results to fully understand their implications is bound to get the session off to a lively start.

Also invite customers, if at all possible, to provide first-hand feedback. Ask them what their priorities are in terms of cost, delivery, performance, and quality and what quality means to them. Engage participants in give-and-take discussions with customers about their requirements, what needs to be done to improve customer satisfaction, and their perceptions of the company relative to competitors. Hearing customer feedback in person is more powerful than looking at charts and graphs.

After they hear the customer satisfaction data, make sure executives ask themselves the tough questions: What do our customers really think of us? Why do they buy from us and not buy from us? What are they happy and unhappy with? What grade do we get in customers' eyes? Are we content with our customers' current level of satisfaction with us? Make every effort to avoid people's natural tendency to dismiss feedback with such comments as "customers are just unhappy in general because of the economy" or "it's only the unhappy customers who ever respond to those surveys anyway." Face the facts as they are known today, and improve survey techniques tomorrow. Capture the results of these discussions for later use.

Competitive Analysis. The second part of the quality assessment is the competitive analysis. The Ernst & Young survey also found that the use of competitive measures by technology-based companies will rise dramatically in the near future. "Three years from now, 45 percent of the companies expect competitor comparison measures to be of 'primary' importance in the strategic planning process. Currently only 18 percent of the companies place that much importance on the competitor measures" (p. 43).

The head of marketing should present a variety of data, ranging from market share and comparative financial results of major competitors to competitors' customer satisfaction ratings and their product and service quality. The financial data are available through quarterly and annual reports, and other data are frequently available through independent customer surveys. Commissioned surveys and personal appraisals may also be necessary to get the full picture.

This part of the quality assessment is important, because executives need to know where they stand in relation to competitors, in addition to gleaning good ideas from competitive practices. Discuss the results of the competitive analysis, and determine the relative strengths and weaknesses of the company and its products and services. Try to identify areas that need to be defended and areas that can be taken advantage of. Creative techniques should be used to facilitate these discussions, such as breaking into subgroups and role-playing customers and competitors. Be sure to capture findings for later use.

Costs of Nonconformance. The third part of the assessment should help executives understand just how much poor quality is currently costing the company—costs that come directly off the bottom line. The discussion should help top managers see, as a corollary, that high quality results in lower costs. Fredrick Smith, CEO of Federal Express, noted with delight, "Recently, we achieved our highest recorded daily service level, 99.7 percent. Just as significantly, on that same day we had our lowest cost per package *ever.* Imagine, the very best service and the lowest cost!" (Federal Express Corporation, 1991, p. 5). It is also significant that Federal Express is able to track its service level percentage and per-package costs on a daily basis.

The expenses traditionally calculated in a cost of nonconformance analysis include internal failures (material scrap and returns, product rework, excess inventories, expediting charges) and external failures (product returns, warranty charges, field service, product liability, accounts receivable delays). Although statistician Lloyd Nelson of Nashua Corporation believes the true costs of poor quality, such as the opportunity costs of lost customers, are "unknown and unknowable," the knowable numbers are high enough to get most executives' attention quickly (Deming, p. 20).

David Kearns (1988), former CEO of Xerox Corporation, estimated the cost of nonconformance to be at least 20 percent of revenues, probably costing the office equipment side of Xerox over $200 million in one year alone. In his words, "one-fourth of all work in American industry is done to correct errors." Phil Kelly, vice president for Motorola, estimated that "the cost of Motorola not having zero defects is at least $800 million a year" (Gill, 1990).

A number of companies have established elaborate systems to capture as many of Nelson's unknowable costs as possible. Such systems are ultimately cumbersome and expensive and are not recommended here. But most companies keep good enough records of their costs to prepare a "quick and dirty" estimate. The benefit of such a presentation is that it can often get a lot of attention. The destructive part is that it can degenerate into a finger-pointing exercise—which must be avoided. The data presented are the responsibility of the entire management team, not just the production, quality, or customer service departments. The lesson to be learned is that poor quality is very expensive and that the company's financial performance can be significantly enhanced through a strategy of improvement.

Employee Satisfaction. Many organizations periodically survey employees' thinking about a broad range of issues, from working conditions to communications and management effectiveness. Although gathered for other purposes, such data are an important component of a complete assessment of the organization's quality position. Are employees proud to work for the organization? Do they respect management, and do they think management respects them? Do employees feel they have management's support in terms of the equipment and training needed to do a good job? Are employees kept well informed about issues that affect them? Do they have channels to communicate their concerns upward to management? Does interdepartmental cooperation exist to effectively solve problems? Are employee suggestions taken seriously and implemented? Do employees think managers are as concerned about quality as they are about costs and schedules?

The answers to questions like these are helpful in deciding how to structure an improvement program to have the greatest likelihood of success. If employees do not think management respects their opinions, they will be disinclined to contribute their ideas on improving quality. Employees who do not trust top management in general will be skeptical and resistant to change.

A broad industry survey of employee opinions conducted by Wyatt Company discovered a number of disturbing facts: only one in three feels encouraged to find new and better ways to work; two-thirds say quality is not an important measure of job performance; a mere 14 percent say they are given a chance to participate in decisions; and only a third say their companies listen to their concerns ("Labor Letter," 1989).

These kinds of employee attitudes certainly do not describe a work environment conducive to improvement. Top management needs to know where it stands with employees before embarking on the quest for quality. If morale and trust are high, an important part of the foundation for quality may already exist. If not, building the leadership foundation must start with employees before any hope for improving customer satisfaction can be realized. "We believe that, when our people are placed first, they will provide the highest possible service, and profits will follow. . . . The bottom line is that, to satisfy our customers, we must first treat our employees as customers" (Smith, 1990). These words should be taken to heart by executives seeking improvement. Unhappy employees are unlikely to beget happy customers.

It should be noted that time-critical issues may be identified during the quality assessment that need to be addressed immediately. In those cases, damage control and problem solving should take place as usual, without a delay to complete the formal planning process. They can be pursued through the normal management channels or special task forces.

Developing a Shared Vision

These four sources of data—customer feedback, competitive analysis, costs of nonconformance, and employee satisfaction—provide the first half of the equation of creative tension, which is a sobering look at today's reality. The other half is a vision of a preferred future. Executives should have been bombarded with enough candid information from the first part of this session to know what they like, what they do not like, and what they want to change. Now that they have looked into the mirror, do they like what they see? If not, then they must define a preferred future. Getting people inspired and working in the same direction must be a high executive priority. What better way to begin than by showing people the "box cover" before asking them to solve the jigsaw puzzle of improvement?

To get participants thinking creatively about vision, ask them to think about what they heard from the four-part quality assessment. What struck them positively and negatively? How would they like to be viewed in the marketplace? It may also be helpful to have them read something in advance about creating a shared vision, like chapters five and six of *The Leadership Challenge* by Kouzes and Posner (1987). Finding an influential supporter in the group to help get the discussion going can also facilitate participation.

The objective of the discussion is to get executives thinking about the future of the organization and their leadership responsibilities. Encourage executives to think freely about the kind of company they want to build for the future. Prompt participants to tackle the tough questions. What are their values, and what do they think is important? How do they want the company to be perceived by customers, employees, stockholders, and suppliers? What will the successful company of the future look like? How can they build on the historical strengths of the company while adapting to an increasingly competitive marketplace? And how can busy executives maintain focus on today's very real business pressures while engaging in a process of continuous improvement and change for the future?

Quality visions can be thoughtful or spontaneous, simple

or complex. During a role-play situation in a weekend training retreat, John Wallace, CEO of 1991 Baldrige Award–winning Wallace Company, stood up suddenly and exclaimed, "Let it be known that from today this company will sell no junk. Every person in the company is empowered to stop any shipment that appears to be junk" (Galagan, 1991b). A quality vision cannot be much simpler or more to the point than that.

For the process to work, normally critical executives must temporarily suspend their judgments about other people's ideas. Assure participants that the more free-ranging and personal the discussions, the better. Peter Senge (1990b) laments, "Today, too many managers want to dispense with the 'vision business' by going off and writing the Official Vision Statement. [Such statements] almost always lack the vitality, freshness, and excitement of a genuine vision that comes from people asking, What do we really want to achieve?" After they share their ideas and feelings with one another, participants can come to consensus on a first draft of a vision that reflects their own deep-seated desires and that will capture people's imaginations.

Organizing the Improvement Steering Council

The final objective of this first session is for the executives to organize themselves as the corporate improvement steering council. Once again, this is not a responsibility that can be delegated. Top managers must invest their personal time and energy to provide leadership for the improvement effort throughout the organization. The council's three primary responsibilities are providing leadership and direction for the effort (Steps 1 and 2 of the improvement strategy); leading, guiding, and supporting the implementation process (Steps 3 through 5); and keeping the implementation strategy and process current with changing business and market conditions (Step 6).

At the conclusion of the first session, the steering council members must agree on what issues need following up prior to the second session and who will be responsible for them. Those issues might range from gathering additional data to refining the first draft of the quality vision. Additional informal meetings may be necessary to reach closure. Participants should also agree on a time frame and location for the next session, and the facilitator should define what prework will be required.

Session 2: Articulating a Shared Improvement Philosophy

Developing a shared quality philosophy that represents top managers' values goes to the heart of Deming's concern for "constancy of purpose." Executives need to share their individual beliefs, biases, and concerns about quality in an open and candid forum. They can often agree on quality goals without even realizing that they disagree about their underlying values and assumptions. The results can be confusing to the rest of the organization and threaten the entire quality effort.

During a second session, a company president insisted that low production yields in the factory had no direct negative impact on the quality of products customers actually experienced in use. He was adamant that defects could be tested out and reworked in the factory and customers would never know the difference. His staff disagreed, insisting that low yields were a sign of out-of-control factory or supplier processes and that no amount of inspecting and testing could screen out all possible defects. As Ray Stata of Analog Devices can attest, "change is blocked unless all of the major decision makers learn together, come to shared beliefs and goals, and are committed to tackle the actions necessary for change" (Kim, 1990). It is essential, therefore, to get these issues out into the open so people know where they stand and where they agree and disagree.

Achieving a shared philosophy, the objective for this second session, is a tricky business that involves the four activities summarized in Figure 2.3.

Determining an Approach for the Session

The thinking of the various quality "gurus" represents different approaches to the subject of quality, summarized in "Resource: Five Influential Quality Philosophies," and each has different

Figure 2.3. Session 2: Articulating a Shared Philosophy.

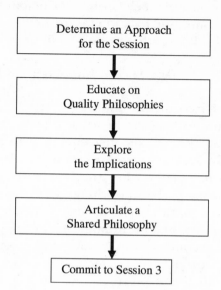

implications for managing the improvement process. The objective of the second session, however, is only to equip top managers with the knowledge they will need to build a leadership foundation, not to turn them into quality experts. Executives demand to have their time well spent, and they quickly grow impatient with quality theories. Prior to the session, therefore, it is advisable to determine what approach will address the subject of quality philosophies most effectively.

A company's quality philosophy usually develops in one of four basic ways:

1. *Unconscious evolution:* A philosophy can unconsciously evolve as a loose set of unspoken assumptions that people are expected to learn as part of their assimilation into the culture of the organization. Articulating a quality philosophy, as advocated here, is an attempt to avoid this approach. A philosophy by default is not a viable way to bring about constructive organizational change. People need to know which behaviors are valued and which are

not. They need to know what is expected of them and how top management wants to run the business.

2. *Selection:* A conscious decision can be made to adopt a particular quality philosophy, such as Crosby's or Deming's. Executives may have had exposure in the past to one or more of the quality gurus and may have a preferred approach. Consultants often have their own preferences. If a clear consensus seems to exist about the most appropriate philosophical foundation for the company, then that approach should be presented in this session and its implications discussed at length by executives.

3. *Conscious evolution:* In a process similar to selecting a philosophy, some organizations begin by adopting a particular philosophy with a plan to let it evolve to become uniquely theirs. This is a practical approach that gets things going quickly and acknowledges the need to remain flexible—as long as this flexibility is not perceived as switching horses in midrace.

4. *Development:* Top managers may be unfamiliar with the different approaches or just decide they need to develop their own consistent with their values. In these cases, executives need broad exposure to the various philosophies, which will let them pick and choose from the best ideas available or give them a common understanding as a point of departure for developing their own approach.

Giving executives the specific education they need requires that you know prior to the session what your objectives are and whether you need to focus on one point of view or on a broader survey of quality philosophies. If a consensus exists about a particular philosophy, build the session around it. If executives are unfamiliar with quality philosophies or simply want to develop their own, structure the session to provide a broader overview.

Educating Executives on Quality Philosophies

Executives can be educated through a variety of means, and someone has to decide whether to accomplish the learning before the session or as part of it. If you plan to focus on a specific approach, such as Deming's, you can have executives attend one of the many outside seminars prior to the session. If attending an outside seminar is not possible, have participants read the work of a quality theorist, such as Deming's *Out of the Crisis,* prior to the session. Either way, participants can come to the session knowledgeable and prepared to discuss the key points of the philosophy and ways to apply it in the company. A more practical alternative often is to have a consultant present a seminar on the particular philosophy as the first part of the session.

The advantage of having executives do their time-consuming learning in advance is that the session can then be shorter. Furthermore, all the time can be spent exploring the implications of the philosophy and ways to apply it. The advantage of educating executives about quality philosophy during the session is that everyone will get the same message and interpret it consistently. The disadvantage of this approach is that the session will have to be longer and less time can be spent on application.

A nationwide study of 130 Business Week 1000 companies discovered that "all companies are not operating under one consistent theory, but rather are blending both internal and external philosophies" (GOAL/QPC Research Committee, 1989b, p. 23). But providing a broad survey to executives who want to develop their own "blended" philosophy can be difficult. There is a strong tendency for consultants and quality instructors to become devotees of a single approach and disparage others. Achieving a well-rounded, unbiased view of the various approaches may require presentations by more than one outside speaker.

Another way to accomplish this with a lot of executive involvement is to have the participants themselves make the presentations. If this seems like a viable option, poll them before the session and determine their willingness to be presenters. Divide the team into groups, and ask them to be responsible for reading up on the works of a particular quality guru and preparing a presentation. One group might select

Deming, another Juran, and another Imai. One of the groups may even choose to research the approach used by another successful company, such as Motorola's six-sigma methodology.

Exploring the Implications

After the basic education on quality philosophies, executives need to explore the implications of the key points. Is the group really in agreement about what the philosophy means and how it will work in practice? If a single approach has been selected, go through the philosophy point by point, testing for agreement about meaning and applicability. For example, many companies adopt Deming's fourteen points, or "principles for transformation of Western management." But in pledging their allegiance to Dr. Deming, do they take the time to really understand each of the points and its implications? Usually not, and the power of Deming's philosophy more often than not becomes lost and further confuses employees.

A quick tour of a few of the fourteen points will demonstrate the problem. Is management prepared to move toward a production system that does not depend on inspection? Are executives willing to forge relationships with suppliers based on mutual loyalty and trust, rather than the lowest purchase price? Do they know to what extent fear pervades the organization and what changes have to be made to eliminate it? Does management really want to eliminate work standards, numerical goals, and merit ratings?

The truth is that Deming's ideals are not only difficult to attain; they are also in conflict with many prevalent assumptions and beliefs about effective management. Top managers should be cautioned not to adopt or espouse a philosophy they do not really understand and are not prepared to support. Take the time during the second session to rigorously evaluate the selected philosophy and make sure it honestly embodies executives' own beliefs and aspirations.

If participants want to develop their own philosophy, they need to look carefully at the elements of a quality philosophy and their personal beliefs relative to each element. The number of possible elements is probably endless, but a starter list should include consideration of relationships with customers, employees, and suppliers, as well as such issues as prevention, continuous improvement, and general management practices.

When beginning to explore and develop a quality philosophy, it is important to obtain maximum involvement from participants. The values expressed in the philosophy must be genuinely theirs, and they must feel complete ownership of the process and the results. An effective way to proceed is to ask participants to review the philosophies presented earlier in the session and to brainstorm a list of elements that they feel should be considered. Combine and prioritize items on the list to come up with a dozen or so key elements. Break into small groups, and have each subgroup focus on one element. Ask them to first write one or two sentences that capture their beliefs or philosophy about each element. Then brainstorm a list of tangible actions, practices, or decisions that would clearly demonstrate and communicate that philosophy to customers, employees, suppliers, and the community.

As an example, part of the philosophy of the Wallace Company, winner of the 1990 Baldrige Award, is to "empower" employees, called associates, to do whatever is necessary to satisfy customers. A tangible policy decision to turn that value into action was to give every associate the authority to make customer-related decisions up to $1,000. As leaders of a "Deming" company, Wallace management also wanted to "drive out fear" and "break down barriers between departments." An effective method for doing both was for John Wallace and his brother to participate in all training retreats for associates. "When you spend a whole day working side by side with an associate on statistical process control it breaks down a lot of barriers" (Galagan, 1991).

Part of the Federal Express "people/service/profit" philosophy is to "consider the effects on our people first in making decisions, recognizing that if we take care of our employees, they will deliver a superior service" (Federal Express Corporation, 1991, p. 3). Tangible actions to support that value include the Federal Express Open Door program, Survey Action program, Guaranteed Fair Treatment policy, and FXTV, one of the largest private television networks in the world to communicate with employees.

These are the kinds of tangible ideas participants need to come up with in the second session to turn their philosophy into a living reality. Ask each group to present its philosophy statement and action list, and try to achieve consensus from the whole group. There should be a lot of give-and-take among participants, and genuine disagreement should be encouraged. Put all ideas to the kind of rigorous challenge they will get later from skeptical employees.

Articulating a Shared Philosophy

The final activity of the second session is to put all this work together and articulate a shared philosophy. Review the points in the philosophy, and make sure all participants agree on the meaning, desirability, and practicality of each. Review the lists of tangible actions needed to demonstrate each point, and make a final "sanity check." Ask participants if they will personally work to support such actions. Encourage them to listen to "the little voice inside" and speak up if they have any reservations or concerns. Challenge participants with organizational examples from the recent past, where their actions, behaviors, or decisions were in conflict with their newly embraced philosophy. Ask them what will be different in the future that will make consistency with the philosophy possible.

After the philosophy has been tested thoroughly, let them work as a group to put it in the form in which they would like it communicated to employees. Final "wordsmithing" is not necessary, but the general format and language should be agreed to. Then ask participants to individually think about actions each of them can begin taking the next day to embody the new quality philosophy. These actions can be large or small, but they must be things that people can and will do on their own without anything else in the organization having to change. After giving them time to think, ask each person to share one or more ideas with the group. It is important for them to commit to themselves and their peers to begin acting consistently with the philosophy. End the meeting by getting everyone to commit to a date for the third session.

Session 3: Selecting a Quality Management System

Initially, executives do not need an in-depth knowledge of the various quality management systems. They need only become sufficiently familiar with them to select an appropriate approach for the organization and make the commitment to begin putting it in place. To help executives become sufficiently knowledgeable to make these decisions, divide the third session into the four major activities shown in Figure 2.4.

Establishing the Need

To gain executive commitment to put a quality management system (QMS) in place, you first have to establish a compelling need for one. Executives have four basic motivations for implementing a QMS: they know they need a framework for improve-

Figure 2.4. Session 3: Selecting a Quality Management System.

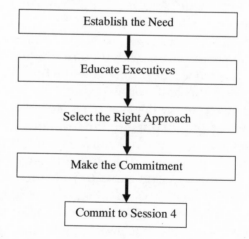

ment, it may be a requirement of doing business, it can serve as a catalyst for improvement, or they seek public recognition. Appealing to one or more of these needs can provide the motivation for implementing a QMS:

• *Framework:* Many companies believe their quality program floundered until they put a QMS in place to structure their improvement activities. Such was the case at Florida Power and Light (FPL). John Hudiburg (1991), its former chairman, says, "Our quest for a new management system began in 1984 when FPL became dissatisfied with its existing quality improvement program. . . . Accordingly, we began to look around for a complete quality management *system,* something much more comprehensive than just teams" (p. 4). After looking at various approaches to quality and finding that "none was the comprehensive system we wanted," he and a group of his key managers visited a number of companies in Japan. They were so impressed by what they achieved that they decided to pursue the Deming Prize and put in place the "companywide total quality management system" practiced in Japan.

• *Business requirement:* A QMS may be a basic requirement of doing business. For example, ISO 9000 certification is increasingly required to do business in Europe and to be a supplier to companies that sell in Europe. If European-related business is an important source of revenue to the company, then ISO 9000 certification is a necessity. Some companies, such as Baldrige Award–winning Motorola, are beginning to drive improvement into their supplier base by requiring suppliers to also apply for the Baldrige Award. Companies that comply with these requirements not only benefit from the additional business they receive but also get a strong quality framework as a bonus.

• *Catalyst:* The third advantage top managers see in putting a QMS in place is that it can serve as a catalyst to get improvement going quickly. Such was the case with Intel Corporation, which referred to its Baldrige Award application as one of the five "transformational events" on its "total quality journey." Intel management felt that the Baldrige criteria and application process served as a "rallying point" and provided part of the focus and direction the improvement process needed. Similarly, certification under ISO 9000 not only provided Conner Peripherals with a structured way to pursue its "Total Quality Commitment," it also served as a catalyst for focusing the organization toward a common goal.

• *Recognition:* The fourth reason companies strive for quality awards, and thereby establish viable QMSs, is for the recognition that accrues to the winners. This recognition is evidenced by the television commercials produced by Baldrige Award–winning companies, such as the Cadillac division of General Motors Corporation. Being recognized as a quality company can positively influence the confidence of the buying public and become a competitive weapon.

A good way for executives to see the need to establish a framework for improvement and understand their own need to be better educated on QMSs is to have them complete a self-assessment. Ask participants to individually complete self-assessment questionnaires based on the Baldrige Award criteria before coming to the seminar. The Quality Consortium, managed by Lakewood Research, publisher of *Training* magazine, has developed just such a survey. The consortium will compile the responses and report the results to the company, along with the national norms established by other companies that have previously participated. Self-assessment or auditing questionnaires also exist for ISO 9000.

The objective of self-assessment is to cause executives to take a hard look at themselves, their organization, and how they manage. Thus they must personally examine and analyze the data. If the group is larger than four or five people, it is helpful to break into small groups to review different portions of the self-assessment. With twelve or more people using the Baldrige Award, for example, you can have four subgroups divide the seven categories of criteria as follows: group 1, "Leadership" and "Human Resource Development and Management"; group 2, "Management of Process Quality" and "Quality and Operational Results"; group 3, "Strategic Quality Planning" and "Information and Analysis"; group 4, "Customer Focus and Satisfaction." Ask them to review their scores and assess the organization's strengths and weaknesses in each category. Have the groups present their findings to one another, and ask if they think the criteria are meaningful to the organization and whether they are happy with how they perceive themselves. If the criteria are important and they believe there is room for improvement, then adopting such a system could be valuable to the company.

Having a management representative from another company talk about how important implementing a QMS was can also be persuasive. Ask the person if the QMS served as a catalyst for improvement and what benefits have accrued to the organization, both internally and externally. Ask whether the company's quality effort would have been as successful, or been accomplished as quickly, without the aid of a QMS. A final appeal can be made to executives' pride by asking the group members whether they would like the company to be recognized as a quality leader. Is there any reason they should not be capable of achieving excellence? Would such recognition not be a competitive advantage in the marketplace?

Educating Executives

Once again, executives do not need to be experts on the subject; they just need to know enough initially to make the right decision and know what it takes to implement a QMS. Consultants, such as an ISO 9000 lead auditor or Baldrige Award examiner, are the most credible and knowledgeable presenters.

New quality awards are constantly being created and revised for the needs of different industries and types of organizations, and it is important to keep abreast of these developments. Those in private industry should be introduced to the ISO 9000 series and the Malcolm Baldrige National Quality Award. Government officials need to understand the President's Award for Quality and Productivity Improvement. Aerospace executives should become familiar with the requirements of the NASA Excellence Award for Quality and Productivity. And executives in the health care industry should be exposed to the

Healthcare Forum/Witt Commitment to Quality Award. Each approach has somewhat different criteria, but they all strive to achieve the same goal: to provide a framework to systematically integrate an organization's improvement efforts.

Selecting the Right Approach

Companies not serving the health care or aerospace markets have a choice between ISO 9000 and the Baldrige Award. Certification under ISO 9000 is ideal for companies that are suppliers to other companies doing business outside the United States, especially in Europe. The Baldrige Award criteria, on the other hand, represent a modern, more comprehensive QMS focused on prevention, customer satisfaction, and continuous improvement. Winning the award should be viewed as secondary to using the criteria as a framework for improvement.

Although most companies can comply with ISO 9000 within twelve to eighteen months, normally a concerted, total quality management effort spanning several years is required to make official application for the Baldrige Award worthwhile. Executives in manufacturing organizations without mature total quality programs should be urged to seriously consider implementing ISO 9000 as a baseline QMS before pursuing the Baldrige Award.

According to the International Standards Organization (1987), "in order to achieve maximum effectiveness and to satisfy customer expectations, it is essential that the quality management system be appropriate to the type of activity and to the product or service being offered" (p. 1). Established QMSs might therefore need to be adapted to specific company needs. An example of adaptation is the way Conner Peripherals developed its QMS. Since the majority of its revenues are derived from international sales, Conner executives committed to the company's becoming an ISO 9000 certified supplier. But management felt the provisions of the standard were insufficient by themselves to meet its customers' needs. After assessing the specific requirements of the computer business and consulting with key customers, Conner developed the "composite" QMS shown in Figure 2.5. Corporate quality policies, ISO 9000, and training serve as the foundation, and the five "pillars" (customer requirements, employee involvement, continuous improvement, statistical process control/critical parameters, and supplier quality management) support the "roof" of total quality commitment.

Making the Commitment

At this juncture, executives have two choices: decide to implement a QMS immediately or wait until later. Before they agree to implement any QMS, people should understand what level of commitment will be required. Even getting certified to ISO 9000, which is a minimal QMS, takes a significant commitment of staff time to do internal assessments, train people, rewrite the quality-related documentation, and make practices consistent with procedures. Implementing the Baldrige Award criteria is a substantially larger effort that requires a great deal of organizational change.

Ideally an organization would implement a QMS to help structure its initial quality efforts. Starting with a QMS means that its implementation can be built into the organization's strategic quality planning and help guide it. But implementing a QMS can also be seen as an additional complication in the early stages of what already seems like a difficult process. The choice to postpone implementation is understandable and may be the best decision in confusing circumstances. At a minimum, do not let the session end without getting a commitment and time frame from participants to revisit the QMS question. Before adjourning, set a date for the fourth session and get agreement on assignments to prepare for the session.

Session 4: Developing the Goals, Strategy, and Plan

In the first session, participants developed a clear picture of the organization's quality position and set overall direction for improvement by creating a shared quality vision. In the second session, they clarified their values and underlying assumptions

Figure 2.5. Conner Quality Management System.

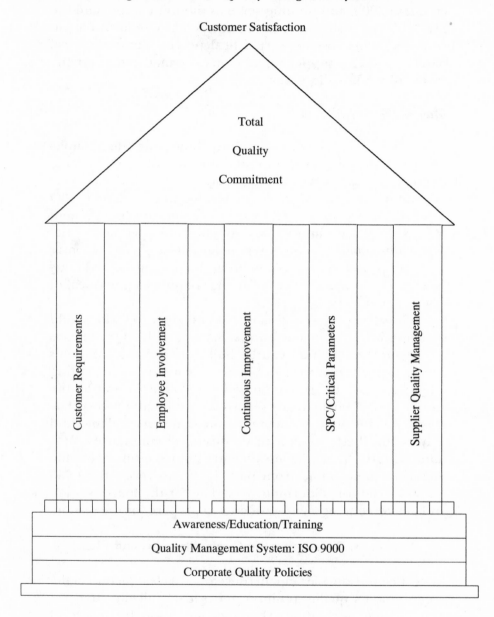

and forged a shared quality philosophy. They selected a quality management system in the third session to provide the framework and integrate the many improvement activities. Having accomplished all this, the team is now well positioned to begin formalizing its strategic quality planning. In the fourth session, executives complete their initial work and training by engaging in the four activities shown in Figure 2.6.

Developing Improvement Goals

Executives should be able to develop an initial set of high-level improvement goals for the company from the results of the quality position assessment conducted in the first session. Once again, it is important to involve participants directly in evaluating the data and in developing goals for the organization that they will be highly motivated to attain. Any method that causes them to critically examine the data and results in a list of preliminary improvement goals will work. One approach that works for larger groups is to break into four subgroups and have each address one of the four sets of data from the assessment. Ask the subgroups to complete the following activities, which will result in four lists of goals where improvement must occur:

• *Customer feedback:* Brainstorm a list of the expectations from the data that are most important to key customers or market segments. What do customers expect from us? What differentiates happy from unhappy customers? What are the few things that really impact customers' decisions to buy from us? Prioritize the list, and reduce it to a dozen or fewer items. Then describe the company's current level of performance next to each expectation and define the performance gap, if any. The performance gap is the difference between what customers desire and the current level of performance. Define a goal that will close each significant gap in performance. Also take into consideration that customers' expectations represent a moving target. Try to get continuous feedback from customers and anticipate what changes are likely. Set target dates for achieving the goals.

Figure 2.6. Session 4: Developing the Goals, Strategy, and Plan.

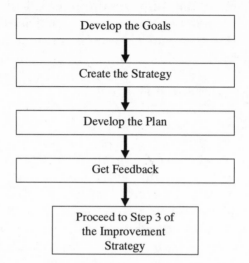

• *Competitive analysis:* Complete a "SWOT" analysis relative to major competitors by identifying strengths, weaknesses, opportunities, and threats. Look at the quality of products and services provided by major competitors, and evaluate their strengths and weaknesses as well as your own. Your strengths or their weaknesses can represent opportunities for increasing market share. Your weaknesses and their strengths can represent future threats. Threats from upstart companies that are not yet viable competitors should also be considered. Brainstorm two lists of goals, one for capitalizing on your strengths and further increasing your competitive advantage and the other for improving your relative weaknesses and protecting yourself from threats. Set milestones for pursuing each goal.

• *Costs of nonconformance:* Evaluate the data on costs of nonconformance, and identify areas where costs are unacceptably high or represent a competitive disadvantage. Develop two lists of goals. The first list is goals for reducing internal failure costs, such as scrap, rework, or expediting expenses. The second list is goals for reducing external failure costs, such as the expenses associated with product returns, warranties, and field service. Brainstorm the major issues related to each, and set target dates for addressing them.

• *Employee satisfaction:* A simple way to evaluate the employee satisfaction data is to array the items on a prioritizing matrix. Label the horizontal axis "Employee Satisfaction," and impose a rating scale that runs from "Low" at the left to "High" at the right. Label the vertical axis "Importance," and impose a rating scale that runs from "Low" at the bottom to "High" at the top. The items that come out on the low end of the satisfaction scale and the high end of the importance scale are of highest importance and should be addressed first. Develop a list of goals for improving the high-priority areas, and make special note of those that may negatively affect the quality improvement process.

Ask the groups to present their findings and discuss their goals. Strive for consensus among participants on the goals and their importance. Have them combine and integrate the goals of the different groups where possible. Complete the initial goal-setting process by prioritizing the lists and reducing them to a manageable number of goals. Remember, these goals will underpin the initial improvement strategy for the organization and will be communicated to employees, suppliers, and customers in the future.

Creating the Strategy

After developing these goals, it is time to begin defining the overall corporate strategy for improvement. One way to start participants thinking about the overall objective is to ask them to read, prior to the second day of the session, the first chapter of this book or a comparable overview of quality strategy. This reading will reinforce the importance of the first two steps of the improvement strategy they have just completed and give them an overview of the steps to follow.

In the large group or in subgroups, participants should discuss applicability of the steps in the strategy to the specific needs of the organization. How do they think the improvement process should be structured to fulfill their quality objectives? What sequence of events will work best in their situation? What elements of the strategy have they already accomplished that can be capitalized on? Brainstorm the kinds of actions and the sequencing that people think will be needed. If subgroups are used, ask them to present their recommendations about how they feel the steps would best be implemented in the company. Integrate the presentations, and come up with a list that summarizes their newly developed strategy, which should capture all the substeps of the six-step improvement strategy.

Developing the Plan

The planning process can be simple or complex. At this preliminary stage, simple is better. The six-step strategy provides a logical sequence for improvement activities and can be used to structure the plan.

Look at the dates of the goals set earlier, and integrate them with the steps in the strategy. Think through realistic dates, and integrate with them the dates for the improvement goals set earlier. Look for scheduling conflicts. Resist the urge to set unrealistic dates; beware again of the hope for "instant pudding." A danger to avoid in planning for improvement is the sense of frustration and failure that comes from people trying to meet unrealistic schedules. Do everyone in the organization a favor when estimating time frames and double the initial estimates. Things always take longer to achieve than we want to believe.

Getting Feedback

Participants should be pleased with themselves for having come this far. When quality programs fail, the root causes can usually be traced directly to trying to push the process down into the organization before a proper leadership foundation has been built. The chances for success are greatly enhanced by completing the first two steps of the strategy before proceeding.

Before communicating the vision, philosophy strategy, and plan to the organization, however, it is a good idea to share it all with others and get some feedback. Develop a plan to "reality test" it with other members of management, key individual contributors, union representatives, suppliers, and customers. To be most effective, the solicitation of input and feedback from other "stakeholders" should really take place throughout the executive training process. Listen closely to their responses, concerns, and suggestions. Ask people if they think the strategy and goals are responsive to the organization's needs. Ask what they think could go wrong and what can be done to help ensure success. Ask if they believe the goals and timetable are realistic. And be sure to ask for their support during implementation.

Get the group together again informally to review this feedback and make changes as required. Pride in authorship of the plan should be secondary to the desire to make it as viable as possible. Once the participants believe that the plan is sound and they have touched all the necessary bases, they are ready to move on to the "awareness" step in the strategy and begin the second phase of training: gaining the understanding and commitment of people throughout the organization.

3

Gaining Understanding and Commitment Throughout the Organization

COMPLETING THE FIRST phase of training helps executives establish the leadership foundation on which all subsequent phases are built. The objectives of Phase 2 training are to bring the thinking of people throughout the organization into alignment with the quality vision and improvement strategy and to gain their understanding of and commitment to the improvement process.

For effective Phase 2 training, executives must establish credibility with middle managers and employees regarding their own commitment to change. The first major credibility hurdle can be surmounted by their demonstrating that they have taken the time to develop a well-considered strategy and plan. The only way to leap the second hurdle is to demonstrate constancy of purpose over time, through sustained, committed action. Too many quality efforts were destined to fail before the journey began because top management tried to rally the employees prematurely, without first defining a destination and charting a course. It is easier for people to find their way in the wilderness if they have a map, and the purpose of the second phase of training is to provide people throughout the organization with a map they can follow with confidence.

Fortunately, much of the groundwork for developing

this training has already been completed in Phase 1. What is left is to package the assessment findings, vision, philosophy, goals, strategy, and plan into training programs and learning experiences for managers and individual contributors. Since the two groups have different roles and responsibilities, the training for them is organized differently and will be discussed separately.

Phase 2 Training for Managers

Managers are responsible for implementing the overall improvement strategy with regard to their specific functions and within their departments. To be effective, Phase 2 training must give them the knowledge and motivation they need to embrace their leadership responsibilities and start down the path of improvement. As with executives, however, dilemmas exist that must be understood and overcome.

Middle management is frequently referred to as a major barrier to improvement rather than the necessary leadership for change. Harvey Kroll, vice president of human resources for Conner Peripherals, reflects that "instead of blazing the quality trail for their people, managers often become the biggest boulders in the path of progress." Why is middle management so often seen as an impediment to improvement? Many reasons are cited. Managers feel threatened by the involvement of employees because it seems to erode their traditional position of authority. They became successful at a time when different skills were required, so they feel insecure and ill equipped to lead the quality effort.

Raymond Sauers, strategist in Ford's Employee Development Office, recounts that when Ford began its participative management approach, "we were confronting managers who were loyal, effective, dedicated people at Ford—managers who had done things a different way, had gotten good results and were quite proud of it" (Geber, 1989). Because they did not understand why changing their historically successful approach would be essential to their continued success, managers at Ford tended to resist the improvement process and work to maintain the status quo.

Beneath these explanations for managerial resistance to change lies another deep-seated concern. Managers see the many contradictions between what executives say and what they do, between how the business is run on a daily basis and top management's professed vision of the future. They get what appear to be conflicting messages: "improve quality" while being measured on volumes, schedules, and costs; "increase employee participation" while not being given the opportunity to participate themselves. They have grown skeptical about what appears to be executives' quixotic interest in passing management fads, feeling they can safely assume "this too shall pass" while they pursue what they know top management really wants: bottom-line results.

Organizing Management Training

Phase 2 training for managers must be organized to overcome their concerns and obtain their understanding and commitment. Managers need to know they have an important role to play. They want to be convinced that top management is really serious about quality. And they need to feel their improvement efforts will be supported and appreciated. The structure and contents of the training must therefore be organized to meet their learning style and needs, and executives themselves must serve as the trainers.

Instructional Team. Training for managers is most effectively conducted by executives, other line managers, in-house quality experts and trainers, and external consultants. Effective programs use all of these resources to form an instructional team. Managers first need to hear directly from executives about the company's improvement philosophy, strategy, and commitment—especially if the spirited pursuit of quality is a departure from the company's past approach. It is a mistake to send in a consultant or staff member to try to convince skeptical managers that the company is now serious about quality; they need to hear that kind of news from the boss.

With executives communicating organizational direction and commitment, other members of the training team can do what they do best. In-house quality staff can provide needed expertise on quality theory and methodology. Internal training staff can provide the instructional design, facilitate the workshop, and effectively debrief the managers following interactive exercises. Trainers can also give executives and other nontraining staff feedback on their presentation skills and provide coaching. External consultants can help structure the workshop materials, provide external perspective and objectivity, share experiences of other clients facing similar situations, and supplement the company's internal expertise in quality.

Program Structure. The initial workshop is best held off-site or at least at a company location that will keep participants from being disturbed by every minor emergency. Larger companies may have suitable in-house training facilities, but most prefer to use a nearby hotel or other off-site facility with the proper learning environment.

Training for managers can be run in a single session of three to five days or be broken into modules. The one-session, immersion approach is simpler to schedule and has the advantage of allowing participants to concentrate uninterrupted on the subject of quality, allowing for reflection and the development of enthusiasm and camaraderie. It is most appropriate for upper-middle managers (Cocheu, 1989). The modular approach divides program content into individual training sessions of six to eight hours. It provides the opportunity for a better transfer of knowledge from the classroom to the job by allowing participants to apply specific concepts at work before moving on to the next subject. The modular approach is ideally suited to first-level managers, supervisors, and individual contributors. Figure 3.1 provides a model of a modular instructional design.

Training Content

The content and instructional materials for the Phase 2 training sessions come directly from the results of the executive training sessions. Whether the single- or multiple-session approach is used, the training content can be broken into the

Figure 3.1. Modular Instructional Design.

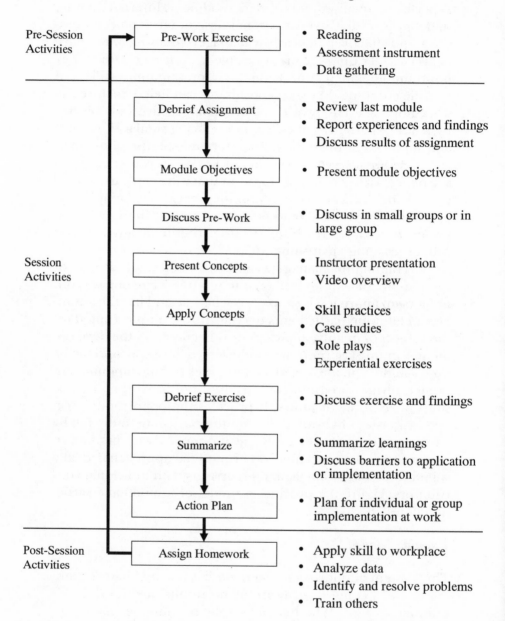

Pre-Session Activities	Pre-Work Exercise	• Reading • Assessment instrument • Data gathering
	Debrief Assignment	• Review last module • Report experiences and findings • Discuss results of assignment
	Module Objectives	• Present module objectives
	Discuss Pre-Work	• Discuss in small groups or in large group
Session Activities	Present Concepts	• Instructor presentation • Video overview
	Apply Concepts	• Skill practices • Case studies • Role plays • Experiential exercises
	Debrief Exercise	• Discuss exercise and findings
	Summarize	• Summarize learnings • Discuss barriers to application or implementation
	Action Plan	• Plan for individual or group implementation at work
Post-Session Activities	Assign Homework	• Apply skill to workplace • Analyze data • Identify and resolve problems • Train others

Source: Cocheu, 1988, p. 13. Used by permission of the publisher.

following four modules, which parallel the executive training conducted in Phase 1: understanding the quality imperative, applying quality principles, implementing quality strategy, and developing improvement goals and plans.

Understanding the Quality Imperative. The content of this module includes an overview of quality's impact on the business, the results of the quality position assessment, and the company's quality vision and future direction. The objective here is to help managers see that rapid and continuous improvement is vital to the company's future. The results of the executives' work on customer satisfaction, competitive analysis, internal cost structure, and employee opinions should be organized into concise presentations and reinforced with interactive exercises that help participants see how the vision was derived from the quality assessment. Make the quality vision tangible and meaningful to managers, and help them see how important their involvement is.

Applying Quality Principles. In the second module, communicate the elements of the quality philosophy and the basic principles of quality. Executive involvement is especially important here when top management's commitment to the improvement philosophy may be questioned. Encourage managers to challenge the concepts and explore their operational implications. Discuss each major point in the quality philosophy in relation to the current way of doing business. Identify areas of consistency between the two, and list them as strengths of the organization. Contradictions should also be pointed out and the discrepancies described. Examples of the behaviors, decisions, and operating procedures that are consistent with the philosophy but different from current practices should be developed and discussed. Encourage managers to speak their minds and question the feasibility of various elements of the quality philosophy. Challenge participants to explore their own insecurities, outdated management styles, and skeptical attitudes, and identify ways they can begin to overcome them.

Implementing Quality Strategy. Present each step in the improvement strategy to show managers how the entire process will proceed. It is important to describe not only the elements of the strategy but also how the steps interrelate and why that specific sequencing is necessary. Have the managers analyze what is involved in each step and what actions they will need to take within their departments. To help participants achieve an understanding of the strategy and its importance, ask them to respond to the following kinds of questions:

- How will they help communicate the quality message and organize the training in Step 3 of the improvement strategy?
- What actions will they need to take to establish an improvement team infrastructure, and how can they start holding individuals responsible for improvement in Step 4?
- How can they get ready to implement a quality management system in their organizations?
- What is the nature of the company's relationship with its suppliers, and what can they do to develop partnerships based on mutual trust in Step 4?
- How do they currently address problems, and to what extent do they really identify root causes and develop solutions to prevent recurrence?
- What problems persist from product to product, or what work processes that interfere with productivity and quality could become candidates for immediate improvement in Step 5?
- How is progress recognized and rewarded in the company, and what can they do to reinforce positive performance more effectively in Step 6?

Developing Improvement Goals and Plans. The objective of this fourth module is to have participants develop specific goals and implementation plans for their own organizations that support the overall company goals and plan. It is important for managers to see the relationship between company-level opportunities for improvement and their own areas of responsibility.

Start out by reviewing the general company goals and plans, and show how they were derived from the findings of the quality assessment conducted by executives in Phase 1. Ask participants to identify the ways that what they do directly or indirectly affects company goals. People often resist drawing these parallels and avoid taking responsibility for global issues they perceive to be outside their control. But be persistent and press participants until they come up with ideas about how their "micro" activities affect the "macro" issues. Once they do, the natural next step is to have them think about what they can do in their organizations to contribute to the accomplishment of the company's goals.

Goals should be oriented toward processes as well as outcomes. Outcome-oriented goals focus on reducing defects, costs, cycle times, and the like. Process goals focus on elements of the strategy, such as developing an improvement team infrastructure, putting a quality management system in place, and organizing the subsequent phases of training. Encourage participants to maintain an approximately equal balance between the two. Planning follows naturally once the goals have been defined. At this point, ask them to estimate time frames that support the accomplishment of the company's plan. Although detailed planning will have to be done by participants back at work, the training will be successful if they leave with initial goals and plans as a starting point.

Phase 2 Training for Individuals

Individual contributors have three major roles to play in the improvement process. The first is to apply quality thinking and techniques to their jobs. It is everyone's responsibility to seek new and better ways of doing things and to bring to management's attention any compromises of quality. People should identify opportunities for improvement in processes, products, and services and seek help when needed to make changes that are beyond their control.

The second role of individuals is to participate as effective members of improvement teams. These teams can be management-directed, such as in task teams, or voluntary, as in quality circles. Individuals should also feel free to form their own teams, as required, to solve problems and improve work processes.

The third responsibility of individuals is to continuously seek greater knowledge and skills in a process of lifelong education. People in every job, in every function, need to continuously learn about new techniques, ideas, and approaches—in the technical aspects of their jobs, in the quality-related skills discussed here, and in general self-improvement.

Learning Objectives

The major learning objectives for individuals are summarized by the title of this phase of training: understanding and commitment. Skills will be developed and specific techniques will be learned in subsequent training phases. In this phase, it is important to establish understanding about the following issues:

- Why quality is important
- What the quality strategy is and why it has been developed
- How it will proceed, what they can expect to see, and when changes will begin to happen
- What roles people will play and what will be expected of them
- What the next four phases of training will be, how they relate to the company's improvement strategy, and why it will be important for everyone to participate

To obtain people's understanding and commitment, the training has to establish management's commitment to quality, instill a sense of urgency to continuously change and improve, and communicate to people that their efforts will be supported and appreciated by management.

Training Approach

Training for individuals is most effectively conducted through a modular instructional design. The subjects can be organized into short, self-contained modules of two to three hours in length, which can be conducted on-site once a week. Modular instruction has two major advantages over the extended workshop approach. From a work scheduling point of view, it minimizes people's time away from work, thereby minimizing the possible negative impact on productivity. From a learning point of view, it maximizes the transfer of knowledge to the job by giving people immediate opportunities to apply what they have learned before going on to the next subject. The immediacy of application has a direct and strong correlation with learning retention.

The Quality Education System developed by Philip Crosby Associates of Winter Park, Florida, is a good example of how to implement a modular design. It contains ten two-hour modules and effectively communicates the Crosby approach to quality. Another example of a good training design is the series of modules recently developed by The Council for Continuous Improvement in San Jose, California. The modules were developed in cooperation with its member companies for use by the members.

Managers, supervisors, engineers, quality assurance professionals, and training department staff can all become effective quality trainers. External consultants who are both knowledgeable about quality and accomplished as trainers can help adapt the training content from managerial training and organize it into a modular format. They can then conduct train-the-trainer workshops for those who volunteered or have been designated for part-time training assignments. The consultants can help the trainers attain a credible understanding about quality while also developing their platform and facilitation skills. Training can be a fun and fulfilling experience for non-expert trainers if they are adequately prepared and if the schedule does not adversely impact their regular work assignments.

Using in-house trainers to deliver the training to individuals has a number of advantages over external consultants:

- It reduces costs considerably.
- In-house trainers can readily adapt the training to learning needs and specific applications within the company.

- They have more credibility because they know the company and its problems better than an external trainer can.
- Conducting the training greatly enhances the trainers' presentation skills and knowledge of quality.
- It makes scheduling and rescheduling much easier.

Training Focus

The content of the training for managers can be condensed into six modules for individuals. Each session should follow the modular instructional design format, using prework assignments, brief presentations of the major concepts, group exercises, and postsession application exercises. The two- to three-hour sessions are only intended to be an overview of the key concepts; in-depth training will be provided in the subsequent phases. Each module is listed below, along with recommended topics:

- *What quality is and why it is important to the company:* quality as a requirement in the global marketplace and as a competitive strategy; customers' concept of quality; business success as measured through customer satisfaction; customers' perceptions of the company's products and services; financial benefits of improved quality; internal customers as the next people in the work process
- *Our quality philosophy, vision, and goals:* the company's quality vision, how it was developed, and the implications for how people do their jobs; the company's philosophy, what it means to the participants, and why it is important; the company's overall improvement goals and how the division or departmental goals support them; what participants need to do as individuals to pursue those goals
- *Our quality strategy, system, and training:* the company's improvement strategy and how it will unfold; overview of the elements in the strategy and what they consist of; what a quality management system is and why it is important; the structure and elements of the company's system; the six-phase training

plan, who should attend the sessions, and what the training schedule will be

- *Teamwork as the key to improvement:* the notion that significant and sustainable improvement is possible only through people working effectively in teams; synergy and how it is achieved; employee involvement and participative management as two sides of the same coin; self-empowerment as a personal responsibility; what improvement teams are, how they work, and what skills will be required
- *Improving processes as a way to make quality happen:* the view that all work can be seen as a series of interrelated processes; process improvement as a precursor to higher quality and customer satisfaction; the concepts of variation and data distribution; what statistical process control is and why and where it is used; how production and business processes are improved
- *How to start making improvement continuous:* improvement as a never-ending journey; next steps in the improvement strategy; what can be expected and how to be prepared; looking for improvement opportunities (fixing things even if they "ain't broke"); where to begin applying the improvement approach on the job; setting individual quality-related performance objectives; developing individual plans for improvement

Phase 2 training is easily developed and will be positively received by managers and individuals if the leadership foundation has been successfully built in Phase 1. The content, which flows directly from the results of executive training, has the legitimacy only top-management's conviction can bring. When effectively conducted, the second phase of training can help people throughout the organization understand what needs to be done and encourage them to enthusiastically pursue it.

4

Implementing a Quality Management System

Everyone received an overview of the organization's quality management system (QMS) in the first two phases of training. In Phase 3, in-depth training begins to start putting the system in place. The overall objectives of this phase are to help people see that a QMS is a present-day necessity of doing business, to show how it helps deploy the quality strategy into the organization, and to give them the knowledge and skills needed to successfully implement the selected system. The ISO 9000 series and the Malcolm Baldrige National Quality Award are the only two QMSs discussed here. Others include the Deming Prize, the NASA Excellence Award for Quality and Productivity, the President's Award for Quality and Productivity Improvement, and the Healthcare Forum/Witt Commitment to Quality Award. The chapter starts with a description of general training for everyone and follows with specific training for managers and project team members.

General Training

The general training that people need to bring the company's policies, procedures, and practices in line with a QMS can be organized into five learning modules: why a QMS is important, principles underlying the QMS, how to use the QMS documents effectively, specific requirements of the selected QMS, and the implementation process. Conducting this training can take from four to eight hours, depending on the needs of specific groups. It should be conducted by an outside expert or an internal person who has been certified as a quality systems auditor.

Why a QMS Is Important

People first need to understand what a QMS is and how it benefits the organization. The International Standards Organization document, *ISO 9004, Quality Management, and Quality System Elements: Guidelines* (1987), is a good resource for this module. It begins by relating the function of a QMS to the goals of the organization: "In order to meet its objectives, the company should organize itself in such a way that the technical, administrative, and human factors affecting the quality of its products and services are under control. All such controls should be oriented towards the reduction, elimination and, most importantly, prevention of quality deficiencies. A quality management system should be developed and implemented for the purpose of accomplishing the objectives set out in the company's quality policies" (p. 1).

The authors of the Baldrige Award also drafted its comprehensive criteria to serve as a foundation on which organizations could build a QMS: "The Award Examination is based upon criteria designed to be a quality excellence standard for organizations seeking the highest levels of overall quality performance and competitiveness. The Examination addresses all key requirements to achieve quality excellence as well as the important relationships among these key requirements. By focusing not only upon the results, but also upon the conditions and processes that lead to results, the Examination offers a framework that can be used by organizations to tailor their systems and processes toward ever-improving quality performance" (National Institute of Standards and Technology, 1990, p. 2).

ISO 9004 goes on to describe the two interrelated functions of a QMS: to serve the needs of the company and to protect the needs of its customers.

> For the company, there is a business need to attain
> and maintain the desired quality at an optimal
> cost; the fulfillment of this quality aspect is related
> to the planned and efficient utilization of the
> technological, human and material resources avail-
> able to the company. [For the customer,] there is
> a need for confidence in the ability of the company
> to deliver the desired quality as well as the consis-
> tent maintenance of that quality. Each of the above
> aspects of a quality management system requires
> objective evidence in the form of information and
> data concerning the quality of the system and the
> quality of a company's products [p. 2].

The discussion of the purpose of a QMS should be followed by a presentation of the reasons why the company decided a QMS is needed. The rationale may be that ISO 9000 not only has become the quality standard for doing business in Europe but also has been adopted in dozens of countries throughout the world. It provides baseline standards that purchasers can contractually require of their suppliers to ensure the integrity of certain aspects of their quality systems. It is important for people to understand that major companies are increasingly requiring their suppliers to become certified under ISO 9000 or to apply for the Baldrige Award as a condition of doing business with them. A letter from a major electronics company, which required ISO 9000 certification from its suppliers, was used to drive home the point to the executives of one firm. The letter began by describing the company's intent to become ISO 9000 certified and stated that a logical extension of its commitment was to drive the certification process into its supplier base. The letter stressed that certification would become an important factor in making decisions and concluded that in the future "any preferred supplier will be required to achieve ISO 9000 certification (or present solid plans to do so)."

Underlying Principles

QMSs are developed by senior quality professionals according to fundamental quality principles. Understanding these underlying principles can not only help people appreciate the basis of their particular QMS but also give them better insight into the improvement process as a whole.

The ISO 9000 series is built on the following elements, which demonstrate the breadth of an effective QMS and the necessity for involving all company functions in its implementation—from top management and marketing to engineering and production:

- Management responsibility
- Quality system principles
- Quality-related costs
- Multifunctional quality involvement
- Control of production
- Product verification
- Control of measurement and test equipment
- Nonconformity
- Corrective action
- Handling and postproduction functions
- Quality documentation and records
- Personnel
- Product safety and liability
- Use of statistical methods

The authors of the Baldrige Award also articulated a number of "key concepts" that underlie its seven examination categories. They provide the conceptual framework to better understand the award criteria. That framework differentiates it from the intentionally more limited scope of ISO 9000. Six of the ten concepts are elaborated in the *1991 Application Guidelines* (National Institute of Standards and Technology, 1990, p. 3):

> - *Customer-driven quality:* Quality is judged by the customer. All product and service attributes that contribute value to the customer, lead to

customer satisfaction, and affect customer preference must be addressed appropriately in quality systems. . . . Customer-driven quality is thus a strategy concept. It demands constant sensitivity to customer and market information and rapid response to requirements. These requirements extend well beyond defect and error reduction, merely meeting specifications, or reducing complaints.

• *Leadership:* A company's senior leaders must create clear quality values, specific goals, and well-defined systems and methods for achieving the goals. The systems and methods need to guide all activities of the company and encourage participation by all employees.

• *Continuous improvement:* Achieving the highest levels of quality and competitiveness requires a well-defined and well-executed approach to continuous improvement of all operations and of all work units of a company. . . . To meet all of these requirements, the process of continuous improvement must contain regular cycles of planning, execution, and evaluation.

• *Fast response:* Meeting customer requirements and expectations and success in competitive markets increasingly demand ever-shorter product and service introduction cycles and more rapid response to customers.

• *Actions based on facts, data, and analysis:* Meeting quality improvement goals of the company requires that actions in setting, controlling, and changing systems and processes be based upon reliable information, data, and analysis. Facts and data needed for quality assessment and quality improvement are of many types, including: customer, product and service performance, operations, market, competitive comparisons, supplier, and employee-related.

- *Participation by all employees:* Meeting the company's quality objectives requires a fully committed, well-trained work force that is encouraged to participate in the company's continuous improvement activities.

Distributing copies of the ISO 9004 or Baldrige Award guidelines to participants and asking them to read selected sections before the session can help expedite the training. Training and orientation materials are also becoming more common, like the two-tape video series produced by the British Standards Institute. This series describes the elements of an effective QMS in general and the specific requirements of ISO 9000. Showing the first videotape of the series and asking participants to describe in their own words what a QMS is and why it is important can help them understand the subject in more practical terms. Another insightful exercise is to have participants rate the company against quality principles to assess its strengths and weaknesses.

How to Use QMS Documents Effectively

Each system has its own documents, and people need to understand how to use them effectively. Participants in Phase 3 training should be given copies of the Baldrige or ISO 9000 documents to use in team exercises.

ISO 9000 Series. The ISO 9000 series consist of three standards, or "models" (9001, 9002, 9003), and two "guides" (9000 and 9004). It is helpful for people to understand that there are different standards for different applications and why the organization decided to pursue the one it did. The standard a company selects depends on the "functional or organizational capacity" required of a supplier by the purchaser. Since participants in the training should already be familiar with ISO 9004, this section of the training should be brief. The following is a summary of the five parts:

ISO 9000: Guide to the selection and use of the ISO 9000 quality standards.

ISO 9001: Standard for quality assurance in design and development, production, installation, and servicing of products. This is clearly the most comprehensive standard; 9002 and 9003 are subsets to assure the quality of more limited functions or capacities. All three are used for external quality assurance in contractual situations.

ISO 9002: Standard for quality assurance in production and installation activities.

ISO 9003: Standard with very limited application—quality assurance only in final inspection and test activities.

ISO 9004: General guide to quality management and quality system elements for internal management purposes.

Baldrige Award. Although the Baldrige Award has one set of criteria for all organizations, unlike the ISO 9000 series, it has separate awards for manufacturing companies, service companies, and small businesses. Up to two awards may be given for each type of organization each year. Whereas ISO 9000 is a pass/not pass system, a point system defines the relative importance of seven broad categories of Baldrige Award examination criteria (with a total of 1,000 points). The seven categories and their point values for 1992 are leadership (90), information and analysis (80), strategic quality planning (60), human resources development and management (150), management of process quality (140), quality and operational results (180), and customer focus and satisfaction (300).

The examination items are scored on three evaluation dimensions: approach, deployment, and results. Understanding these dimensions is important because they can be applied to the overall improvement strategy, in addition to the QMS:

Approach: The methods the company uses to achieve the purposes addressed in the examination items (appropriateness of tools to requirements, effectiveness of the use of tools, prevention orientation, system integration, and use of quantitative information)

Deployment: Extent to which the approaches are applied to all relevant areas and activities addressed and implied in the examination items (application to all products and services and to all transactions with customer, suppliers, and the public)

Results: Outcomes and effects in achieving the purposes addressed and implied in the examination items (demonstrated quality levels, rate and breadth of improvement, sustained improvement, comparison with industry and world leaders)

Requirements of the Selected QMS

People need to become familiar with the specific criteria of the QMS, where the company stands in relation to the criteria, and the requirements for compliance.

ISO 9000 Series. Certification under ISO 9000 essentially requires a company to address two main questions: Does the company have a comprehensive set of policies and procedures that cover the quality-related activities and functions defined by ISO, and does the company systematically comply with its own policies and procedures? George Lofgren (1991), president of the Registrar Accreditation Board, advises companies: "The assessors look for objective evidence that the supplier is conforming to its own documented procedures and that the procedures meet the intent of the standard."

Preparing to become an ISO 9000 certified supplier requires a company to take four main steps: audit existing documentation against the ISO standard, update the documentation to meet the intent of the standard, audit conformance of practices to the documentation, and correct nonconformances. To take the first step, people in the organization need to become familiar with the requirements of the relevant quality standard. ISO 9001, for instance, includes eighteen quality systems requirements, ranging from contract review and design control to process control and training.

An effective technique to help participants explore the meaning of the elements and apply them to their organization is an informal self-assessment. Participants can rate the company against each element on a simple three-point scale: +1 for strengths, 0 for neutral, and –1 for weaknesses. Such an assessment stimulates lively discussions and helps people come to a common understanding of the standard in relation to the organization.

The limitations of ISO 9000 are many: compared with the Baldrige Award, it emphasizes traditional, inspection-oriented practices rather than prevention activities; it does not address the need for continuous improvement; and it focuses on compliance with policies and procedures rather than on quality results and customer satisfaction. However, becoming an ISO 9000 supplier exposes people to quality-related disciplines and gives them the experience of working together cooperatively. It can serve as a good foundation. Many companies would be well advised to start with ISO 9000 before thinking seriously about trying to measure up to the demanding Baldrige Award criteria.

Baldrige Award. To become familiar with the Baldrige criteria, participants should be encouraged to conduct an informal self-assessment of the organization. They can do an exercise like the one described for ISO 9000 or use one of the commercially available questionnaires. As mentioned in Chapter Two, the Quality Consortium, managed by Lakewood Research, has two versions: an extensive version for managers and an abbreviated one for others. Other companies provide surveys that can be self-scored. ASQC Quality Press and Quality Resources publishes a *Quality Management Benchmark Assessment* (1991) that integrates both the ISO 9000 and Baldrige criteria. Once again, the self-assessment process helps people learn about the QMS and understand the criteria in a fun and interesting way.

It is not sufficient, however, to become knowledgeable about the individual Baldrige Award scoring criteria, because they form a truly integrated system. People must also understand the relationships among the criteria. For example, Category 3.0, Strategic Quality Planning, requires a company to define major quality goals and strategies and plans for achieving them. Category 4.0, Human Resource Utilization, cross-references these planning requirements by asking the company to describe how the company's "recognition, promotion, compensation, reward, and feedback approaches for individuals and groups, including managers, support the company's quality and performance objectives" (National Institute . . . , 1991, p. 19). The lesson is that a company must have not only quality objectives but also the means to measure, recognize, and reward performance in relation to those objectives.

Another example of the interrelated nature of the Baldrige criteria involves Category 6.0, Quality Results, which asks the company to summarize "trends and current levels for all key [internal] measures of product and service quality" (p. 15). Category 7.0, Customer Satisfaction, asks for the reporting of "trends and current levels in indicators of customer satisfaction for products and services" (p. 19). The lesson here is that improvements in a company's internal quality measures are not sufficient by themselves; they must be accompanied by corresponding improvements in customer satisfaction.

These interrelationships among examination categories necessitate a correspondingly high level of interorganizational coordination and cooperation—a major challenge to even the most effectively managed companies. Participants should be challenged to discover other such interrelationships and to identify barriers that could frustrate efforts to cooperate across organizational lines.

Implementation Process

The final piece of general training that everyone needs is exposure to the implementation process. The QMS project team is responsible for developing a detailed implementation plan for the company. The team works closely with management and other significant contributors throughout the organization to assess organizational effectiveness and to develop a plan that has broad commitment.

The QMS implementation process, which serves as the foundation of the implementation plan, can be broken into three groups of activities: preaudit, audit, and postaudit. Understanding how the process works facilitates detailed planning. Participants should be asked to review the process and identify potential roadblocks and actions they can individually take to prepare for implementation. The generic process described here can be used as a general implementation guide for both ISO 9000 and Baldrige Award systems:

Preaudit activities:
1. Educate top management and establish commitment.
2. Organize the project team.
3. Train project team members.
4. Develop an implementation plan and schedule.
5. Establish responsibilities throughout the organization.
6. Provide QMS awareness training for the organization.
7. Conduct a formal self-assessment audit of the organization.
8. Provide feedback to departments and management.
9. Develop and implement corrective action plans.
10. Train people in new policies, procedures, and work instructions.
11. Confirm compliance and readiness.
12. Select a registrar and schedule an audit (ISO 9000 users), or submit eligibility and application forms (Baldrige Award users).

Audit activities:
1. Have an outside agency review the quality documentation for consistency with ISO requirements (for ISO 9000 users), or evaluate the application in relation to competitors (for Baldrige Award users).
2. Schedule and conduct an on-site audit or examination.
3. Accept the audit report issued by the agency (for ISO 9000 users).

Postaudit activities:

1. Fix nonconformities, and have corrective actions verified prior to being granted certification (for ISO 9000 users).
2. Have the agency issue ISO certification (for ISO 9000 users) or notification of status and feedback reports (for Baldrige Award users).
3. Maintain a system for periodic third-party surveillance (for ISO 9000 users), or maintain and improve the QMS (for Baldrige Award winners) or reapply next year (for losers).

Training for Specific Groups

Beyond the general subjects everyone is exposed to, managers and project team members need additional training to support their specific responsibilities in implementing the QMS.

Management Training

Management support and leadership are required if people are to dedicate the necessary time and resources to QMS implementation. It is up to management to encourage teamwork and break down barriers that traditionally get in the way of interorganizational cooperation, which is the lifeblood of any QMS. The following additional management training can take between four and eight hours, depending on participants' existing knowledge:

- Using the QMS to reinforce and support the company's overall improvement strategy and plans
- Using the QMS as a foundation on which to build a total quality management approach
- Providing leadership and obtaining interorganizational cooperation
- Assessing and allocating resources
- Making the commitment to succeed

Managers should discuss how the selected QMS relates to the company's existing quality strategy and how the two can work together to reinforce a total quality management approach. They need to discuss the requirement for inter-organizational coordination and identify barriers to cooperation as well as opportunities for overcoming them. It can also be very useful to invite a speaker from another company who has experience implementing the selected QMS to give an overview of the process and describe what makes it work. "War stories" are always effective in getting people's attention and helping them apply theory to the workplace. This discussion should lead participants to identify likely barriers to implementation in the company, develop possible countermeasures, and individually identify specific actions they can take to get the process rolling.

Project Team Training

The implementation team is composed of responsible individuals who can effectively represent their functions or organizations and provide the leadership needed to obtain broad support and cooperation. All major functions should be represented on the team. Project team members need to be sufficiently knowledgeable about the QMS implementation process to conduct training and perform preaudit self-assessments within their organizations.

These responsibilities require team members to be trained as quality system auditors. This training is best conducted by a recognized external agency, such as the British Standards Institute (BSI), or by an experienced consulting firm. BSI conducts five-day Lead Auditor Training courses periodically in locations around the country and the world. These courses combine in-depth training on the ISO 9000 series with training in quality auditing techniques and procedures. Courses on preparing to apply for the Baldrige Award abound from recognized consultants, many of whom have served as award examiners or senior examiners.

The following general outline is representative of the subjects covered in courses for ISO 9000 project team members:

- Introduction to quality system auditing
- In-depth understanding of ISO 9000 series requirements
- Quality terminology
- Auditing principles and techniques
- The quality auditing system
- Quality system implementation planning
- Alignment of quality system documentation (policies, operating procedures, and work instructions)
- Preparation and scheduling for self-assessment
- Conduct of self-assessment
- How to give feedback and issue noncompliance forms or corrective action reports
- Verification of corrective actions and closeout of noncompliances
- Preparation for external audit
- Leadership and monitoring of postaudit corrective actions
- Maintenance of the system for ongoing third-party surveillance

The auditing training provided by external sources is usually practical and applied. The presentation of each major concept is followed by what are called "workshops" or "syndicated activities." During these workshops, participants work in small groups to apply what they have learned to realistic case studies. Participants then present the findings or results to the entire class and are given constructive feedback. They are normally given the opportunity to take an optional examination to demonstrate their knowledge of quality system auditing. The results of such examinations can be used as the basis for recognition and certification within the company. Additional courses—on such important subjects as leadership, interpersonal skills, project management, negotiations, constructive feedback, and teamwork—can also be helpful to project team members.

5

Empowering Improvement Teams

SUCCEEDING IN THE struggle for improvement requires the applied creativity, passionate concern, and skillful performance of everyone in the organization, working together toward common goals. With a strong improvement team infrastructure, a company can deploy its improvement strategy, marshal the energies of its people, and organize a coordinated response.

Like Chapter Four, this chapter is organized by the types of training that different people need. The general training that everyone should be exposed to is described first, followed by specific training for improvement team leaders and managers. These discussions are preceded by descriptions of two approaches to training—"just-in-time" and "task-applied" training—that will help ensure skills are effectively transferred from the classroom to the job.

Choosing a Training Approach

The ultimate objective of any training is to give the right people the right knowledge and skills at the right times to help them do "the right things right." But the traditional "spray and pray" approach to industrial training has not always had this result. In this approach, people are randomly brought together in a classroom, given theoretical knowledge, and sent back into the workplace with the hope that they will be able to apply the knowledge and improve things. The experiences of one organization after another have been disappointing. Sending people to class does not by itself result in the application of learning to the job.

Training must be integrated with quality strategy to facilitate its implementation. Strategy provides the context and meaning for the training, and the training provides the knowledge and skills people need to put the strategy into action. But training must also be better integrated with actual performance. People learn by doing, and they learn best when the training helps them accomplish things they are already trying to do. The way to ensure that what is learned is applied to the job is to use "just-in-time" and "task-applied" training approaches. Both require people to participate in training in teams, not as isolated individuals. Team members acquire a common understanding and become capable of applying what they learn at the same time. A supportive work environment that has the "critical mass" needed for group action is essential if people are to effectively apply their newly learned skills.

The three things to keep in mind when organizing training are to shorten the delay between training and the application of the skills; train people in their teams, not as individuals; and try to incorporate training with the actual performance of team tasks whenever possible.

Just-in-Time (JIT) Training

Traditional training is unrelated in time to the performance of a specific task; the hope is that people will know what to do whenever the occasion arises. JIT training, on the other hand, is timed to provide people with specific knowledge and skills just before they will need to use them. Since people's ability to retain what is learned and to effectively apply it drops off dramatically as the length of time between the training and the opportunity to use it increases, it is important to structure the training flexibly, so it can be delivered just in time. For example, it is more effective to teach people problem-solving skills immediately before they are required to solve a problem than it is to have them attend a class weeks or months before.

Shortening the delay between training and performance greatly increases people's ability and motivation to apply what they have learned. But JIT training requires close communication among the team, the management, and the instructors to anticipate a team's need for certain skills and to coordinate the delivery of training. Although it is difficult to predict exactly when teams will need training on specific skills, teams usually develop in similar ways and require new skills in a similar order. For example, teams need to learn how to run a meeting before they can solve a problem, and they need to understand the problem-solving process prior to learning how to use quality tools. Short, skill-specific learning modules offer the greatest flexibility. Such modules are very focused and normally last from one to four hours, depending on the subject. The modular instructional design shown in Chapter Three is an example of how to structure training in this way.

Task-Applied Training (TAT)

TAT is similar to the JIT approach but goes a step further: it incorporates the training into actual performance of the task. For instance, a team that is formed to address a specific customer satisfaction issue, like incorrect invoices, is taught the problem-solving process as part of its regular team meetings. The team members learn the process and then apply it to their specific situation. Next, they need to know how to gather data systematically to obtain the information they need. Then team members need to learn how to analyze the data they collect. Training continues in such steps until they have solved the problem and learned all the skills in the process. Long-time quality consultant Stanley Marash says, "The only way to make a process successful is to teach it for a couple of hours once a week and then work on implementation over a period of time until people learn how to use what they have been taught" (Stratton, 1990b).

Since teams are a means of deploying the organization's improvement strategy, training is best provided to teams after they have been given management direction and are in the process of trying to fulfill their charters. By ensuring the immediate application of skills to the business problem at hand, TAT builds retention and provides visible bottom-line results. Training done in this way is viewed as an enabler of business results and not as a questionable overhead expense.

Participating in Teams

"A quiet revolution is taking place in many organizations. The source of the revolution is the growing realization that tighter controls, greater pressure, more clearly defined jobs, and tighter supervision have, in the last fifty years, run their course in their ability to give us the productivity gains we require to compete effectively in the world marketplace. Attention is shifting," says Peter Block (1991, p. xvii), "to the need for employees to personally take responsibility for the success of our businesses if we hope to survive and prosper."

Completing this revolution requires changing traditional attitudes and acquiring new skills. On the attitude side, managers and individuals must address the issue of their own "empowerment," a much overused and misunderstood concept. On the skills side, people need to develop or enhance a variety of skills, ranging from working effectively in meetings to solving problems and making decisions. The following five subjects should be taught to everyone who is involved with improvement teams: self-empowerment, meeting management, team organization, problem solving and decision making, and quality tools.

Training for upper-level managers and team leaders is normally delivered in a three- to five-day seminar scheduled just as teams are being formed. It is difficult to break managerial training into JIT learning modules; team leaders need the broad overview and intensive learning experience provided in a seminar. But training for supervisors and team members is best organized into separate learning modules and delivered through a JIT or TAT approach.

Team leaders are best trained by external consultants who can also teach them to deliver the training to team members. The best source of training for managers depends on their level. First- and second-level managers can be taught by external consultants or by experienced internal staff trainers who receive external training along with team leaders. The training of higher-level managers is usually left to external consultants, as discussed in Chapter Two.

Although everyone needs exposure to all five subjects, different groups require more or less emphasis, depending on their roles in the improvement team process. The different emphasis required for managers, team leaders, and team members is summarized in Table 5.1.

Self-Empowerment

The key to improving is not so much mastering specific skills and techniques as it is believing that we, as individuals, can and must make a difference, that we have more control of our own destiny than we are often aware of or care to admit. Most of us know that customers provide the revenue that pays our salaries and that happy customers are preferable to disappointed ones. People intuitively understand that it would be easier to do things right the first time rather than do them over and over. And we would rather find the root cause of a problem and solve it once than face the problem again and again.

Table 5.1. Team Skills Matrix.

Skill	Managers	Leaders	Members
Self-empowerment	3	3	3
Meeting management	2	4	3
Team organization	4	2	2
Problem solving and decision making	3	4	3
Quality tools	2	4	3
Leadership of improvement teams	3	3	1
Creation of an empowering environment	3	2	1

Note: 1 = not initially necessary, 2 = overview, 3 = ability to use, 4 = ability to train others.

If we already know all this at some level, why don't we act as if we do? In great part we do not because the problems we face appear larger than we are and we feel powerless to change things. This feeling can affect vice presidents as well as individual contributors. When we feel powerless, the natural tendency is to look to our management to tell us what to do or to give us permission to act. But as Block points out, "this waiting for the gods to decide, and blaming them for not deciding, is in itself a symptom of the problem" (p. xviii). People at all levels know when the defect rate is too high and customer satisfaction is waning; they don't need to be told by the company president.

Each person in the organization, regardless of position or job title, knows when things are going wrong and has ideas about how to make things better. Each of us must initiate actions to do what we know is right without having to be told—out of obligation to ourselves, if not to our customers or to the organization. We need to maintain our own sense of integrity, to feel good about ourselves and not feel compromised by politics, indifference, or bureaucracy.

Such self-empowerment is a fundamentally different concept from the paternalistic "employee involvement" approach so popular today. Empowerment is not a technique, and it is not something that is done to or for people. It is something that we must do for ourselves. It is a decision that each of us makes every day about how we want to live our lives. True, some organizations make it safer for people to take responsibility for what they believe is right. But improvement always means change, and change is always risky. The question is how we individually and collectively react in the face of that risk, which is increasingly part of our fast-paced work environment.

"Teaching" people how to take personal responsibility for their work lives and for the success of the enterprise is not a well-developed science. The first objective is to have people realize that direction from above is insufficient by itself to make quality happen; each of us must take the risk on a daily basis to do what we know is right for customers and the organization.

The second objective is to have people confront the reasons for their own feelings of resignation or powerlessness and commit to taking greater personal responsibility.

How important is empowerment training, and how can you tell whether your organization needs it? The best way to answer these questions is to ask several others. Do people in your organization trust management, take risks to say what they think, and demonstrate initiative to make things better? Do you get a feeling of enthusiasm and excitement when people talk about what they do? Do they regularly share ideas with management about how to improve things? Do they come up with improvement goals and ideas for new projects on their own, without being asked? Do people work well across functions and cooperate with one another? Do they focus on solving problems without trying to place blame? Do they see the company's customers as their own and do whatever is necessary to satisfy them?

If the answers to these questions are generally positive, then people may already be well on their way to feeling empowered. In this case, you may not need to spend a lot of time on the subject or go into in-depth training. A good example of the kind of conceptual overview of empowerment that might be appropriate in this situation is Peter Block's *Empowered Manager* book and videotape. You can show the video and use the leader's guide to facilitate a discussion of the key points. Distribute the book and assign the first three chapters for prework reading. Asking participants to highlight quotes or passages they find particularly interesting or applicable can stimulate a lively and worthwhile discussion. Having them discuss situations in which they felt empowered or unempowered can also lead them to better understand their own responses to situations and to the conditions that foster feelings of empowerment or powerlessness.

If the answers to the preceding questions are generally negative, which is true more often than not, then a more intensive training approach might be advisable. A good example is Stephen Covey's *Seven Basic Habits of Highly Effective People* (1989), available as a book, audiotape, and multiday training seminar. His experiential approach is popular and effective for team training.

Covey demonstrates how productive teamwork moves through a three-stage process, from dependence to independence to interdependence. The first step, from a state of emotional dependence to independence, involves three skills or "habits": being proactive, beginning with the end in mind, and putting first things first (pp. 48–52). Having attained independence, where they take responsibility for their actions and cease blaming forces outside themselves, people can begin to develop the three habits of interdependence: thinking win-win; seeking first to understand, then to be understood; and synergizing. The seventh habit, "sharpening the saw," involves continuous self-improvement in all aspects of our lives.

Regardless of the approach used, it is critical to help people understand that, in addition to leadership from above, self-empowerment of the individual is the other necessary force of change. Rapid, continuous improvement requires that we take responsibility for doing what we believe is right and working collectively toward that goal.

Meeting Management

Teams can achieve their objectives only if they work effectively. Since working in teams involves meetings, team members must learn effective meeting management skills. People frequently complain that meetings are frustrating, unproductive, and a poor use of their scarce time. This can be as true for the executive steering council as for improvement team meetings.

One or more of the following shortcomings are usually mentioned when people are asked to describe a typical meeting in their company:

- An agenda and objectives are lacking.
- People go off on tangents, and discussions become unfocused.
- Nobody keeps the discussions and agenda on track.
- Meetings take too long and never get to the key issues.

- Some people always dominate and shut out other points of view.
- People come unprepared and waste everyone's time.
- Issues are brought up but not resolved.
- Action items get lost, and people are not held accountable.

These all-too-familiar symptoms result from not defining how the meeting will be conducted—the meeting process—and not clarifying what people's responsibilities should be—meeting management roles. The meeting process and roles are discussed first, followed by suggestions for training.

Meeting Process. Working in teams is much easier when a framework or process is established that everyone understands and agrees to use. People then do not have to struggle with the meeting process and can concentrate on the subject of the meeting.

Although meetings can have a variety of purposes, they should all have a similar structure. The example shown in Figure 5.1 has four stages:

1. *Preparation:* Organizing the logistics (time, place, equipment), defining the meeting objectives, developing the agenda, communicating in advance with team members, and completing all necessary prework.
2. *Opening:* Stating the meeting purpose, the objectives to be accomplished, and expected outcomes. Meeting purposes include informing, solving problems, making decisions, generating ideas, and selling ideas or decisions. Aligning people's expectations with the purpose of the meeting enables participants to interact appropriately. The agenda should be reviewed to see if people are in agreement and modified to meet the needs of the team.
3. *Body:* Presenting and discussing each agenda item. Relevant data should be concisely presented, differences of opinion brought to the surface, decisions made, follow-up actions identified, and clear responsibilities assigned.

Figure 5.1. Effective Meeting Process.

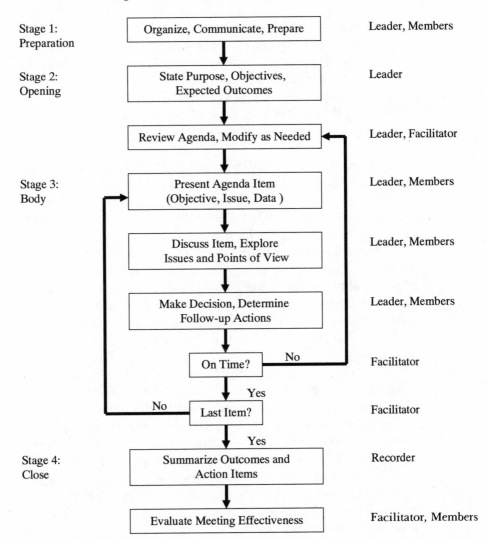

Stage 1: Preparation	Organize, Communicate, Prepare	Leader, Members
Stage 2: Opening	State Purpose, Objectives, Expected Outcomes	Leader
	Review Agenda, Modify as Needed	Leader, Facilitator
Stage 3: Body	Present Agenda Item (Objective, Issue, Data)	Leader, Members
	Discuss Item, Explore Issues and Points of View	Leader, Members
	Make Decision, Determine Follow-up Actions	Leader, Members
	On Time?	Facilitator
	Last Item?	Facilitator
Stage 4: Close	Summarize Outcomes and Action Items	Recorder
	Evaluate Meeting Effectiveness	Facilitator, Members

The time should be checked periodically to see if the meeting is on track, and the agenda should be adjusted as agreed to by the team.

4. *Close:* Summarizing the outcomes and action items and verifying people's understanding of the proceedings after all agenda items have been covered. Like all other activities, team meetings should be continuously improved by evaluating their effectiveness and identifying opportunities for enhancement.

Meeting Roles. In addition to learning about a clear meeting process that everyone can follow, people need to learn how to carry out different roles in meetings to keep meetings focused and on track. There are four essential meeting management roles that apply in all situations:

• *Meeting leader:* The person who calls the meeting (either the team leader or one of the team members) and takes responsibility for organizing and conducting it. The meeting leader focuses on the content of the meeting rather than the meeting "process," which is the facilitator's job. The meeting leader's job is to ensure that the objectives of the meeting are accomplished.

• *Facilitator:* The meeting facilitator can be anyone on the team (the responsibility should be rotated regularly) who manages the meeting process. The meeting leader is like the passenger in a limousine, and the facilitator is the chauffeur. The passenger determines the destination for the trip, and the chauffeur takes care of the details of getting there on schedule. Relieved of this responsibility, the meeting leader can concentrate on the issues. The facilitator, on the other hand, does not get involved in the issues or voice opinions in the discussions. This role distinction is critical, because it is difficult to be personally involved in the content of a meeting while keeping an objective eye on the meeting process. The facilitator's role is the most important, most difficult, and most overlooked ingredient in running meetings effectively.

• *Recorder:* The team "scribe," who keeps track of decisions, agreements, and action items. It is easy for important points to be forgotten or overlooked in the heat of discussion. The recorder also summarizes the outcomes and action items at the end of meetings to ensure that accountability for follow-up actions is clear. Although the recorder is not prohibited from actively participating in the discussions, as the facilitator is, recording is difficult to do well if the person gets personally involved in the issues.

• *Member:* Responsibilities include coming to meetings prepared and on time, engaging actively in discussions, dealing with the issues and not taking criticisms or alternative views personally, keeping the welfare of the team in mind at all times, giving and receiving constructive feedback, and respecting other people's roles.

Training. Meeting management skills are introduced early in team training so they can be used for all subsequent team meetings. Like many skills, they are best learned by doing. A good way to begin is to present the meeting process and roles in the initial team meeting and then to apply them during the rest of the meeting. Ask people to volunteer for the four roles. Define the objectives of the meeting, develop an agenda, and complete the meeting. Ask the team at the conclusion to provide feedback to the leader, facilitator, and recorder. Discuss what went well and how the meeting could have been improved. Close by asking participants to select a meeting leader and facilitator for the next team meeting, and seek their agreement to use an established meeting process in the future.

Publish the agenda prior to the next team meeting, and again proceed through all four stages. Ask the team to give the facilitator latitude to manage the meeting process. During the closing stage of the meeting, evaluate the effectiveness of the meeting and compare it to similar meetings in the past. Ask the team to give the meeting leader, facilitator, and recorder positive feedback and constructive suggestions for improvement (another person will have to facilitate this feedback discussion). Rotate responsibilities for the next meeting, and incorporate the process into all future team meetings. If you do, people's meeting management skills will evolve naturally over time.

Team Organization

Effectively deploying the corporate improvement strategy throughout the organization means using different types of teams at all levels and coordinating the efforts of all team activities to achieve common goals. Everyone involved in team activities needs to understand when to use the different types of teams and how teams are set up. Suggestions for training follow the discussion of these subjects.

Types of Teams. The types of teams that organizations use range from the corporate improvement steering council to quality circles, and they all have different functions. Depending on their mission, teams can be temporary or ongoing in nature. They may be composed of people within a specific function or department or from different functions or organizational units. These are some typical kinds of teams:

• *Corporate and division steering committee:* Provides direction and coordination for the improvement process; composed of senior managers who are in charge of major functions or departments.

• *Project management team:* For example, an ISO 9000 implementation team, which leads and coordinates the organization's initial efforts to become certified. Team members represent key functions and departments throughout the organization. After the team has accomplished its mission, it can disband and delegate ongoing oversight responsibilities for the project to the steering committee or to departmental teams.

• *Business process improvement team:* Cross-functional team that works to improve business processes cutting across organizational lines. For example, since a single department seldom has the knowledge or authority to improve such a complex business process as new-product introduction, cooperation is needed from marketing, product engineering, and manufacturing. These teams can function at any level of the organization.

• *Quality circle:* Popular form of employee involvement team in the United States since the 1970s, when it was "imported" from Japan. Membership is voluntary, and team members typically work in the same department or in closely associated work groups. A quality circle tends to meet once a week for an hour or so to identify areas for improvement, analyze problems, and seek approval from management to implement solutions.

• *Process improvement team:* Different from a quality circle in several important ways. Membership and participation are not voluntary; they are an expected part of regular job duties. Members of a process improvement team are usually from the same department or function, and the team can act as an extension of the division steering council, doing the data collection, analysis, and implementation. Such a team tends to be better integrated into the overall improvement strategy and process than a quality circle is.

• *Problem-solving team:* Tends to be problem-specific and of limited duration; organized any time the solution of an immediate problem is beyond the regular organization or process improvement teams. The focus of problem-solving teams is initially problem containment. The objective is to minimize the impact of quality problems on the customer and to give the organization time to put in place a long-term solution.

Team Setup. The efforts of all these teams must be focused toward implementation of the company's improvement strategy and accomplishment of corporate-level goals. Direction and information need to flow from level to level and organization to organization. The quality vision, philosophy, goals, strategy, and plans developed by the corporate steering committee must flow down through the division steering councils to the improvement teams. Likewise, feedback and information must flow back through the chain to create a closed-loop communications system, as shown in Figure 5.2.

An example of an effective team infrastructure is the "TQC structure" at Boeing Military Airplanes (BMA). In 1981, BMA started a quality circle program to increase employee involvement. But in 1986, after "five years of fragmented but worthwhile activity" behind them, management realized they lacked the "connectedness between organizations, and be-

Figure 5.2. Improvement Team Infrastructure.

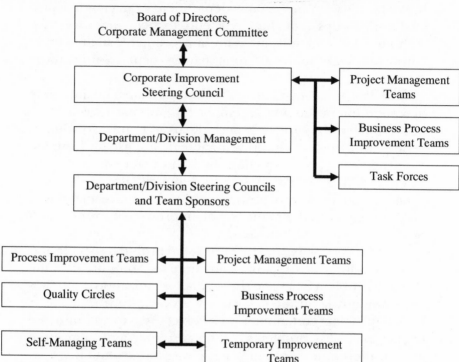

tween management and workers, needed to make significant, measurable gains in cross-functional processes" (Klusman, 1989). In their new TQC structure, teams begin at the executive level with the president and his staff (composing the quality council) and are formed at all levels down to quality circles. The BMA "quality council" and "lead teams" guide the activities of "quality improvement teams" and identify problems to be worked on by "task teams." According to Cathy Klusman, "the first step toward that new environment was to train employees in TQC roles. Team leader, team member and facilitator classes provide basic instruction in the use of problem identification and problem solving tools and techniques, as well as in teamwork and group dynamics."

Once steering councils have been formed at the corporate and division levels and have established the necessary leadership foundation, the next step is to begin creating a flexible, dynamic team structure throughout the organization. This effort should build on whatever team-related activities are currently in progress and enhance them to involve as many segments of the organization as possible. For example, if quality circles have already been established, their efforts should be integrated with the overall improvement strategy, and they can become full-fledged process improvement teams.

When setting up and chartering teams, regardless of type or mission, be sure to clarify management's expectations. The following are typical questions that must be answered early when forming teams: What exactly are the desired outcomes of team activities? How will the team's progress be measured—how can the team tell if it is succeeding or not? How will the steering committee and improvement teams communicate? Will regular, two-way communication be possible? Is the team intended to be temporary or to have ongoing responsibilities? Will there be time restrictions on team meetings and other related activities? How should team members prioritize their regular job duties with those required by the team?

It is up to the individual teams to get organized and begin to pursue the company's goals. Developing a vision or mission statement is a popular initial activity for teams. Although it may be useful for ongoing teams, it is often impractical for temporary ones. In any case, teams must quickly identify tangible goals and timetables for their activities. The relationship between their goals and those of the division and corporate councils should be clear. Asking for management confirmation can also help clarify the charter and prevent misunderstandings. Training teams in meeting management skills also helps them start quickly.

Training. After presenting the information about team organization at an initial team meeting, review the specific team charter provided by management and note areas that need clarification. Ask participants to make sure they agree on the purpose of the team and determine what type of team is most appropriate under the circumstances. Should it be temporary or ongoing? Should it be limited to people within a department, or would it be more effective with participation from other functions?

Proceed to develop a preliminary set of goals for the team. Start by reviewing the goals, strategies, and plans developed by the corporate and division councils. After defining the goals, try to identify some time frames for completing the initial activities. Make sure to use the team meeting process to guide the discussion, and communicate the team's goals and plans to the appropriate managers.

Participants may also benefit from identifying the different types of teams the organization is currently using or has used in the recent past. Have them evaluate the effectiveness of those team efforts. What made some teams effective? What should teams avoid doing in the future? These lists of do's and don'ts can be used to develop a set of guidelines or operating principles that the team can follow. Assess which portions of the overall improvement team infrastructure are currently in place in the organization and how well they are working. Any ideas for improving the overall infrastructure should be relayed to the steering council for consideration.

Problem Solving and Decision Making

Problem solving is the lifeblood of improvement, and every team needs a tool kit of techniques for solving problems, making decisions, and putting corrective actions in place. Group problem solving and decision making are much more effective when team members understand and agree to use common, structured approaches. Examples of such problem-solving and decision-making approaches, and ways to teach people to use them, are described in this section. These two processes are closely related and should be taught together.

Problem-Solving Process. Since solving problems is part of daily life, we tend to think we are naturally good at it. The difficulty with teaching effective problem solving, therefore, lies not so much in having people learn the process as in helping people question their assumptions, overcome some of their natural tendencies, and maintain the discipline necessary to work effectively in teams. People often assume that everyone on the team has a common understanding of the problem, even when no formal definition has been articulated. The urge to discuss solutions before the cause of the problem has been determined is equally strong. People also tend to implement a newfound solution and assume that it eliminates the problem without verifying its actual effectiveness.

The nine-step process shown in Figure 5.3 is simple to understand, and learning to use it consistently in teams will help overcome these all-too-common problems.

1. *Organize team:* Put a team in place with the appropriate people. Involving the right people with the right skills is critical to solving problems and implementing solutions effectively.
2. *Describe problem or improvement opportunity:* Develop a concise statement of the problem or improvement opportunity that all team members agree with. Avoid the urge to jump over this step, and get a common definition in writing before proceeding.
3. *Gather and organize data:* Information is the key to effective problem solving. The tendency to discuss people's opinions without supporting data often wastes a great deal of time.
4. *Contain problem:* Identifying the root cause of the problem and developing a solution can be time-consuming, and the interests of the customer may have to be protected in the meantime. For example, the root cause of a product defect may not be knowable immediately. It could be attributable to a supplier problem, an out-of-control process, or a design-related issue. An inspection or testing procedure may have to be put in place to contain the problem and minimize the possible negative impact on a customer in the short term.
5. *Identify root cause(s):* This critical step involves sorting out problem symptoms and identifying root causes. The common tendency to focus on symptoms ensures that problems will recur; eliminating problems means find-

Figure 5.3. Problem-Solving Process.

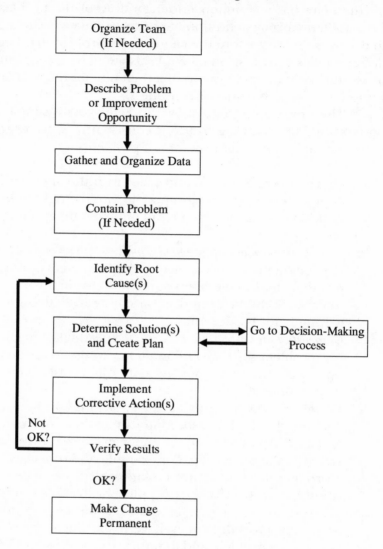

ing and fixing root causes. Buying a new battery for a car when it will not start, for example, does little good if the root cause is a faulty electrical system. Lowering the price of a product may not increase sales if the customer perceives the problem to be inferior quality or poor service.

6. *Determine solution and create plan:* The solution most likely to eliminate the root cause of the problem and prevent its recurrence must be determined. Finding the optimal solution requires use of the decision-making process discussed later. Discovery of the solution is followed by development of a plan to implement the necessary corrective actions. Implementation may require management approval, additional resources, or cooperation from people outside the team. The means to measure the impact of the solution should also be considered.

7. *Implement corrective action(s):* Determining the solution is often easier than implementing it. Cooperation among all involved parties must be obtained, and corrective actions must be put in place in an orderly way that will enable the impact to be measured.

8. *Verify results:* The means to measure the impact of corrective actions must be put in place simultaneously with their implementation. It should never be assumed that the first attempted solution will actually eliminate the problem. Thinking of the process as an experiment is helpful: the effects of altering certain variables while holding others constant are measured and compared against the desired result. If the solution does not provide the desired result, then the root cause, solution, and implementation should be reexamined.

9. *Make change permanent:* Once the solution has been verified, it needs to be documented, communicated, and systematically implemented as a permanent change to current operating practices. This step includes communicating the solution to other operations or divisions and retraining people as necessary.

Decision-Making Process. Decisions can be made as part of the problem-solving process or separately from it. Selecting a movie to go to, for example, is simply a decision to be made—because no problem exists. But identifying the best solution among a number of alternatives for eliminating a product defect is a decision step within the overall problem-solving process.

Making decisions in a team setting is best accomplished when team members understand and agree to use a common framework. The seven-step process shown in Figure 5.4 should be taught in conjunction with problem solving.

1. *State purpose of decision:* A clear statement of the purpose in decision making is as important as clearly defining the nature of a problem. An example of the importance of a clear purpose was illustrated by a company that mounted a campaign within its sales organization to increase revenues. The catchy phrase "Revenue is everybody's business" was used by the sales executive to rally the troops. When the sales managers sat down to decide what to do, however, they were not sure what the purpose of their decision was. Was it really just to increase revenue, or was it actually to increase market share? Or should increasing revenue be a means of indirectly improving profits? The lack of a clear purpose led to unnecessary confusion.
2. *Establish criteria and priorities:* If the purpose of the decision was simply to increase revenue, how much revenue would make for a successful campaign? Could the increase in revenue be accomplished by lowering prices to raise volumes? How low could they go? Would it be acceptable to try a solution that decreased overall profitability? If so, how much of a decrease would be acceptable? Could the increase in revenue be accompanied by increases in costs for advertising and promotion? Once again, how much would be too much? The answers to these kinds of questions become the criteria for weighing the alternatives and judging the decision. Once the criteria are set, it is important to determine priorities. Is

Figure 5.4. Decision-Making Process.

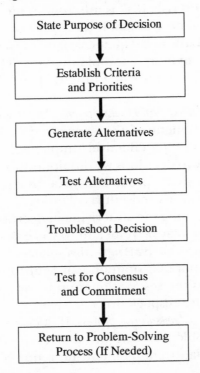

it more important to maintain current pricing or to keep costs down? Ranking or weighting the criteria according to their relative importance is a way to test alternative solutions.

3. *Generate alternatives:* People tend to lock onto a single idea or possible solution without exploring the alternatives. Avoid this problem by encouraging people to think creatively and not rush the process. Generate as many ideas as possible, and suspend judgment until later.

4. *Test alternatives:* The judgment that was suspended when generating the alternatives must now be invoked in testing them. All reasonable alternatives should be evaluated to see which best meets the prioritized criteria. The alternatives can be rated independently or ranked collectively.

5. *Troubleshoot decision:* Even the best decisions may be fraught with risk. Risk is inherent in life and in business and cannot be avoided. But the risks should be carefully examined, the consequences of error weighed, and contingencies explored and planned for. There is no sense being surprised by something that could have been anticipated.

6. *Test for consensus and commitment:* Any decision must have the commitment of those involved to help ensure its chances of being effectively implemented. We have all been party to decisions we did not fully support, and the results are always predictable. Halfhearted commitment leads to halfhearted efforts. Testing for consensus can require probing for underlying concerns or reservations that people may be reluctant to voice publicly. As in the classic movie *Twelve Angry Men,* near-consensus and the weight of popular opinion can lead to unfortunate results unless the reservations and beliefs of even a single dissenter are respected.

7. *Return to problem-solving process:* If decision making is part of the problem-solving process, then return to it and create a plan to implement the required corrective actions.

Training. The problem-solving and decision-making processes, like meeting management, can best be taught using the JIT or TAT approach. The most effective method is to first introduce a simple but realistic case study. Start by giving team members an overview of the processes and let them work their way through each step. When participants get to the "determine solution" step, they may need coaching through the decision-making process. If small subgroups are used in the training, it is best to have them formalize their work from each step and present it to the class. This gives people a chance to develop their presentation skills.

The case study will familiarize people with the processes, which is the first objective of the training. Then team members will be ready to apply the processes to a real problem they need to solve. The TAT method works best in this situation if two classroom sessions are scheduled; people need time to collect data between the first and second sessions. End the first session after participants have developed a written description of the problem, and give them an assignment to go back and collect the necessary data. They should come to the next session prepared to present their data and proceed to work their way through the remaining steps of both processes. Once again, the need to present their findings motivates participants to do a thorough job and lets them develop their presentation skills. It also provides an opportunity for people to provide and receive feedback, which are important skills for working in teams.

Quality Tools

Most people have been exposed to one or more of the many "quality tools." These tools, popularized by the quality circle movement, are used within the problem-solving and decision-making processes to help team members do everything from gathering information and organizing it to reaching consensus and planning action. The power of these simple tools and the central role they play in all team activities cannot be overstated. They can be used competently by anyone in any position with minimal training. Although originally used primarily on the factory floor, their use is of equal value in office or customer service settings.

In Table 5.2, the various tools are categorized by the functions they serve. Control charts, which are traditionally included in lists of quality tools, are reserved for the next chapter, where their role in process control and improvement will be demonstrated. It is important to develop competence and confidence in applying these basic techniques before introducing people to statistical process control methods.

Teaching people to use quality tools should be done on a JIT or TAT basis. People should be taught these skills as the need to use them arises to ensure a smooth transfer of learning to the workplace. As an example, checksheets, which provide a simple way to gather data, can be introduced in conjunction

Table 5.2. Quality Tools.

Tools	Functions
Brainstorming	Generating ideas
Checksheets, run charts, interviews, surveys	Gathering data
Graphs	Displaying data
Histograms	Showing frequency distribution
Pareto charts	Prioritizing data
Cause and effect diagrams, scattergrams, force-field analyses	Determining relationships
Process flow charts	Understanding processes
Multivoting, nominal group technique	Reaching consensus
Gantt charts, PERT charts	Project planning

with the third step in the problem-solving process, where gathering and organizing data are required. The use of histograms, which display the distribution of data, and Pareto charts, which display data in frequency order, can be taught to people to help them organize their information. Cause and effect diagrams can also be taught, to help focus the data-gathering effort, or can be taught later, along with scattergrams, when people are trying to identify the root cause of a problem. These are simply a few examples that demonstrate how the use of quality tools can be taught in conjunction with problem solving in order to ensure the maximum transfer of learning to the job.

Leading Improvement Teams

Team leaders need to acquire a number of skills beyond those required by regular team members, since they are responsible not only for leading the teams but also for training team members. It is advisable that team leaders receive their training from external consultants who specialize in improvement team training. Any number of team leader courses are available. They normally run from three to five days in length. The training is intensive and highly interactive, with participants having to complete day and evening assignments, engage in various role-play situations, and make numerous group presentations. The added benefit of using external training sources is that they often have fully developed course materials for use in training team members back on the job.

Larger organizations will also want to get their regular training staff trained at the same time. The most effective training of team members occurs when team leaders, who have operational responsibilities and experience, co-teach with professional in-house trainers, who already have good instructional skills. Sharing responsibility lets the team leader focus on the operational and technical issues in the training and lets the trainer focus on facilitation and group dynamics. Trainers can also coach team leaders to improve their presentation and facilitation skills.

The additional skills normally included in team leader training, beyond those already described, fall into seven broad categories:

> *Demonstrating leadership:* Providing vision and direction that inspire the interest and enthusiasm of team members, developing an empowering environment that encourages creativity and risk taking, and communicating confidently and nondefensively
>
> *Facilitating group interaction:* Keeping the team on track, minimizing dysfunctional behavior, eliciting the full participation of team members, and maintaining a positive, productive climate
>
> *Negotiating differences and resolving conflict:* Being able to focus on group processes, rather than getting involved in the issues themselves, and facilitating win-win solutions or agreements that are positive for all parties involved
>
> *Training team members:* Providing team members with the skills they need on a JIT or TAT basis
>
> *Coaching for improved performance:* Diagnosing team members' strengths and weaknesses, giving them positive reinforcement for their accomplishments, providing constructive feedback for areas needing development, and serving as a role model for others to follow
>
> *Presenting ideas persuasively:* Understanding the audience

and organizing and presenting information to achieve
the desired goal

Building management support: Communicating effectively
with various levels of management; keeping management abreast of progress, problems, and resource
requirements; and constantly linking team activities to
organizational improvement goals and priorities

Creating an Empowering Environment

Managers are responsible for creating a work environment that
fosters feelings of empowerment and individual responsibility
in others. From a structural point of view, it is management's
job to set up improvement steering councils to lead the improvement process, to follow the lead of executives at the
corporate level, and to move team activities down through
divisions and departments. Linking the councils and the improvement teams is essential to effectively deploying the
company's strategy, goals, and plans. A leadership foundation
must be built by managers at every level of the organization.
Without management direction from the steering council,
teams are destined to fail—as many ill-fated quality circle programs have demonstrated.

From a personal point of view, managers need to can-
didly assess the level of their own empowerment. The conditions that create emotional dependence and impede
empowerment can affect anyone at any level. It is easy to feel
that the troubles of the organization are larger than life and
beyond any individual's power to influence or control. Managers' first responsibility is to overcome their own feelings of
powerlessness and apathy. We all need to look inside before we
blame others for the problems we face. Unempowered managers stand little chance of encouraging their people to become
more personally accountable for the success of the organization.

Creating an empowering work environment also requires
developing a participative management style that encourages
active employee involvement. When Donald Petersen, chairman of Ford Motor Company, was asked how Ford changed

from its entrenched way of thinking to a process of continual improvement, he responded:

> The initiation of employee involvement as a concept, and now a way of life, was certainly a major help. . . . But first we had to do something to allow change to happen. For us that took the form of a companion effort in participative management. We needed to change the "now-hear-this" mentality, the notion that an employee should listen carefully and not think too much. To ask for employees' ideas without first building management's receptivity would be to drive those ideas right into a brick wall. The effort of changing to participative management has taken and still takes a lot of effort in training and education because we're having to change managers who have succeeded by a different route. We not only want them to change to participative management but to believe that it is a better way. That's the harder part of the process [Galagan, 1988].

Fortunately, management attitudes toward employee involvement are changing rapidly. When executives were asked in a recent survey, conducted by *Electronic Business* and Ernst & Young, what they considered the most effective method to improve product quality, the most frequent response (76 percent) was "employee involvement" (Baatz, 1991). This change in philosophy, from a "now-hear-this" philosophy to a participative one, is a bigger leap for some managers than others. It takes sensitivity to know how to organize their training most effectively.

Training to help managers feel empowered and develop a more participative style of management is usually best left to external consultants or highly experienced internal trainers. Effective approaches include the Stephen Covey program, mentioned earlier, and the Leadership Challenge program conducted by the Tom Peters Group. The Leadership Challenge program is based on the research of James Kouzes and Barry Posner (1987). The authors insist that leaders functioning at their personal best demonstrate the following five leadership practices:

- Challenging the process by confronting the status quo, experimenting, and taking risks
- Inspiring a shared vision by envisioning the future and attracting others to common purposes
- Enabling others to act by fostering collaboration and sharing power and information
- Modeling the way by setting the example and planning small wins
- Encouraging the heart by recognizing contributions and celebrating accomplishments

These kinds of programs have several things in common. Participants get feedback from others they work with through confidential questionnaires to get perspective on their behaviors and management styles. Seeing themselves as others see them can stimulate the desire to change the ways they work with others. Another commonality is that these seminars are frequently organized as retreats, where participants live together for several days and become immersed in the experience. Training of this sort is also highly participative and experiential, frequently including outdoor exercises to build trust and teamwork. Regardless of the specific training approach used, however, the objectives are the same: to get managers to make a candid assessment of their management styles and openly consider the value of alternative approaches that can elicit greater commitment from the people they manage.

6

Improving Production and Business Processes

ONCE PEOPLE HAVE learned to work effectively in teams to solve problems and make decisions, they are prepared to learn more sophisticated skills for controlling and improving processes (Phase 5 training). One of the most common mistakes organizations make is to train people on statistical process control before the improvement team infrastructure has been built to support its use. When the infrastructure and skills are developed first, people are able to apply process control and improvement techniques immediately, achieve quick results, and build confidence for continued application.

The two principal methods people need to learn to conduct improvement projects are statistical process control (SPC) and business process improvement (BPI). Although SPC has been most commonly used in manufacturing and production environments, the underlying concepts can be applied in other settings to any repetitive work process. SPC has been around for many years and is at the heart of product quality improvements throughout the world.

More recently, organizations have also begun to see the tremendous potential of improving everyday business processes and support services, which people often take for granted. Business processes, such as new-product development, cut across many disciplines and departments and are often enormously wasteful. They normally go unattended because no one appears to "own" them and they seem to be beyond any one person's influence. Likewise, support services, such as purchasing or engineering documentation, are also often ignored, even though their effectiveness or efficiency can significantly aid the operations they support.

In this chapter, the process management concepts that underlie SPC and BPI are discussed first, followed by an overview of both these techniques and a discussion of the training needed to begin using them.

Process Management Concepts

Everyone from the executive suite to the showroom floor needs to grasp the basic concepts that underlie all process control and improvement tools. The two overall learning objectives of this module of Phase 5 are to prepare people to shift their attention and resources from dealing with problems to preventing them and to help people see that appropriate decisions cannot be made without understanding the fundamentals of variation.

Training in process management concepts can be organized as a single workshop conducted just before implementation of process control and improvement activities. Use simple examples from daily life to communicate the four basic concepts—prevention, variation, process capability, and methodology—and bring in job-related examples to drive the points home. The most effective instructor of these concepts is someone who has both hands-on experience controlling and improving processes and experience managing projects and people. Teaming an internal SPC expert with a trainer or external consultant is often the best approach.

Prevention

Quality improvement requires moving toward prevention activities, such as SPC, and away from after-the-fact inspection and problem solving. Prevention requires controlling work processes, not simply measuring and reacting to their results.

Process control, which strives to identify variation and its causes, is the only way to prevent defects from occurring. Measures like counting manufacturing scrap, field returns, or customer complaints occur too late in the process to do anything about them; the errors and dissatisfaction have already taken place and the added costs incurred. It is far better to move "upstream" and control the process before the defects are generated.

Using seat belts when driving and getting flu shots in the winter are everyday examples of prevention activities. Unnecessary automotive injuries and debilitating flu symptoms are the unfortunate consequences of not practicing prevention. Numerous familiar examples from the workplace can also be used to demonstrate the need for prevention. Ask participants to brainstorm recent situations where the use of prevention practices would have saved time and money. People enjoy the exercise and can always come up with a long list of examples, because hindsight is always more acute than foresight. Training is successful when participants understand that preventing problems or defects is simpler and cheaper than finding and fixing them. They can then start thinking creatively about how to incorporate more prevention practices into their work.

Variation

W. Edwards Deming (1982) stresses: "The central problem of management in all its aspects . . . is to understand better the meaning of variation, and to extract the information contained in variation" (p. 20). Variation is the primary enemy of quality, and understanding variation is essential to controlling and improving processes. "A fault in the interpretation of observations, seen everywhere," Deming continues, "is to suppose that every event (defect, mistake, accident) is attributable to someone, or is related to some specific event. The fact is that most troubles with service and production lie in the system. Confusion between common causes and special causes leads to frustration of everyone, and leads to greater variability and higher costs, exactly contrary to what is needed" (pp. 314–315).

"Special" causes of variation are those that can be attributed to sources outside the process that influence the output of the process but are not part of the process itself, such as variations in the quality of incoming material. Special causes of variation can be reduced without changing the process, and they must be eliminated before statistical control can be achieved. A process that contains special causes of variation is by definition not in a state of statistical control.

"Common" causes of variation are predictable and inherent in the nature and design of the process—such as the capability of a piece of equipment. In Deming's terms, they are part of the "system." If left to itself without influence from any outside source, any process will produce some level of variation due to common causes. A process with only common causes of variation is said to be in a state of statistical control. The level of variation due to common causes cannot be reduced without changing or redesigning the process. Treating common causes of variation as if they were special, what Deming calls "tampering," inevitably leads to increased rather than decreased variation.

The appropriate responses to common and special causes of variation are summarized in Table 6.1.

A classic instructional technique used to demonstrate tampering (treating common causes of variation as if they are special) is dropping marbles through two funnels from the same distance onto paper targets on the floor. One funnel is held in place without movement, and identical marbles are spun around the inside of the funnel, one at a time, and allowed to drop onto the target. The landing location of each marble is marked. The position of the other funnel is constantly adjusted after each marble is dropped in an attempt to get the marbles to drop closer to the center of the target (a form of tampering).

Moving the second funnel around actually increases the size of the pattern—exhibiting a combination of common and special causes of variation. The pattern produced by dropping marbles through the first funnel is smaller and more predictable; it demonstrates the effect of common causes of variation. If the system itself is changed, by moving the funnel closer to

Table 6.1. Variation: Sources and Responses.

Actions, Sources, and Consequences	Process Not in Statistical Control	Process in Statistical Control
Sources of variation	Common and special causes	Common causes
Appropriate actions	Investigate special causes	Change system
Consequences	Identify and eliminate special causes—resulting in a state of statistical control	Reduce common causes of variation—resulting in improved process capability
Inappropriate actions	Treat special causes as if they are common (change system in response to special causes)	Treat common causes as if they are special (attempt to eliminate variation that is inherent in the system without changing the system itself)
Consequences	Wasted resources	"Tampering" and increased variation

the target, the pattern becomes even smaller. Marbles of different sizes can also be dropped through the funnels to demonstrate the effects of a special cause of variation; smaller marbles create a wider pattern than larger marbles do. Standardizing marble size eliminates the special cause and creates a predictable pattern of variation. Participants should be encouraged to identify and discuss work-related examples to see how variation affects every process—including their own.

Process Capability

Every process has a specific capability or tolerance. This tolerance is the variation due solely to common causes and is independent of the specification tolerance or customer requirement. A process may or may not be capable of producing results that meet requirements, even when in a state of statistical control. Simply speaking, a process with a tolerance, due to common cause variation, that is larger than specified is incapable of meeting customer needs consistently. It must be purposefully changed to reduce common causes of variation.

An everyday example most people can relate to is the fit of their clothes. Consider weight, or waist size, as the process and clothing size as the specification tolerance. Everyone's weight varies a little from day to day, but our clothes still fit relatively comfortably. We can say that our process tolerance, or the amount our weight varies, is within the specification tolerance of our clothes. But as we grow older, our metabolism slows and we exercise less. We begin to put on weight, and our process tolerance no longer fits comfortably within the specification tolerance of our clothes. When that happens, we have two options: we can either lose weight through diet and exercise (reduce process variation) or wear a larger size of clothing (change the specification tolerance).

Another example is the express lunch service featured in many restaurants. The restaurant guarantees that lunch will be served within ten minutes and even provides a timer at the table to keep track. If the lunch is not delivered within ten minutes, the customer gets a free dessert. Because ten minutes is the specification tolerance, the restaurant has to make sure that the tolerance of the overall ordering-cooking-serving process is also ten minutes or less. When it is, customers receive the service they expect, and the restaurant does not have to give away any desserts.

Numerous examples comparing process tolerances to specification tolerances can also be drawn from work. Such an example from the electronics industry is the precision of a component insertion machine (process tolerance) compared with the spacing and diameters specified for the holes on a printed circuit board (specification tolerance). Participants should be encouraged to brainstorm a list of such examples from their jobs and identify processes that might be incapable of performing within specification. These examples can be used later in the training.

Methodology

Many organizations go through an initial period of SPC implementation in which people feverishly "control chart" numerous processes, only to be disappointed with the lack of results.
What is missing is a methodology or structured approach to
controlling and improving processes. Such was the case with
the Uniroyal Goodrich Tire Plant, in Fort Wayne, Michigan.
They began their SPC effort by training employees throughout
the factory on control charting techniques, only to realize that
"a change in direction was needed." By following a structured
"SPC approach that we developed, we have come to better
understand our operations. Rather than merely establishing a
charting system that identifies changes in the system, we have
been able to eliminate some causes of waste" (Cantello,
Chalmers, and Evans, 1990).

    As with problem solving and decision making, both SPC
and BPI require structured approaches to be effective. Although the two approaches vary somewhat to accommodate
the differences in the environments in which they are applied,
both can be reduced to simple, step-by-step models. Introduce
both SPC and BPI by presenting the models and their applications, to provide the necessary conceptual framework, before
starting training on the specific tools and techniques.

Statistical Process Control

Variation is the enemy of quality, and SPC is the foremost method for controlling variation. Common barriers to effective SPC
training are discussed first, followed by descriptions of an SPC
model and the corresponding training.

Barriers to SPC Training

Courses on SPC abound these days, with sources ranging from
professional associations and statistical consultants to local

colleges. Therefore, teaching people the technical skills is relatively easy. However, people frequently encounter three types of barriers when they try to learn and apply SPC: personal, instructional, and organizational.

Personal Barrier. The most common barrier is that many people have limited math skills. SPC requires the ability to perform basic functions, such as calculating averages and percentages. If the people who are to be trained in SPC have difficulty with simple math, it is a good idea to focus first on improving their math skills. It is better to avoid the embarrassment and frustration that can result from proceeding too quickly. Community colleges are an excellent source of help in testing people's levels of mathematical attainment and providing remedial math education at very reasonable costs.

Instructional Barrier. People often struggle with SPC instruction when the initial emphasis is on the math rather than the underlying concepts. It is easier for people to learn how to use specific techniques if they first see the "big picture" and understand the basic logic. The concepts of prevention, variation, and process capability can be taught by building on the simple team skills covered in Phase 4 training. The SPC trainer should make sure the conceptual framework and logic are understood and internalized before teaching statistical techniques. Evaluate the training provided through outside consultants or the use of purchased materials to make sure proper emphasis is placed on building a solid conceptual understanding.

Organizational Barrier. The organizational barrier people frequently face is the lack of an SPC implementation plan. Without a plan or immediate requirement for SPC, people lack the motivation to learn and see training as a frustrating waste of time. And without the ability to apply what they have learned, people do not have the opportunity to build practical skills and quickly forget what they were taught. SPC training should be taught just in time or, even better, using the task-applied training method. Do not start until a solid implementation plan has been developed.

SPC Model

Before people learn the technical aspects of SPC, they need to understand the logic and flow of the overall approach to controlling processes shown in Figure 6.1. It is within such an approach that the various tools and techniques will be used, including run charts, control charts, gauge repeatability and reproducibility, and capability studies. The nine-step model is a generic approach that can be used on any process that is a candidate for SPC.

SPC Steps 1–3. The first step is to determine the customer requirement, which is usually stated in the form of a specification by the customer or product designer. The next two steps identify the elements of the product or service that affect the requirement and the key quality characteristics of the element.

Consider an example from the disk drive industry. One of the product elements that can influence the read/write consistency of a hard disk drive is the disk/motor subassembly. The key quality characteristic of the disk/motor assembly is the vibration or "warbling" that can result from imbalance of the disk on the motor spindle. Table 6.2 shows the typical questions that should be asked at these steps (and the other six steps), as well as the conclusions and actions that result.

SPC Steps 4–5. The work processes that determine the key quality characteristic are then defined. In the example, they are the disk mounting and balancing processes. The processes should be documented, flow-charted, and validated. Process validation entails checking to see that process documentation accurately reflects the process in use and resolving any discrepancies. A measurement system must then be established.

The Uniroyal Goodrich plant discovered that "a major shortcoming of many SPC programs has been the failure to assess the measurement tools used to determine product quality. . . . It has been a common assumption that the measurement system is satisfactory. This assumption proves to be incorrect in many cases. Checking the ability to make measurements is an important building block for all subsequent SPC

Figure 6.1. Statistical Process Control Model.

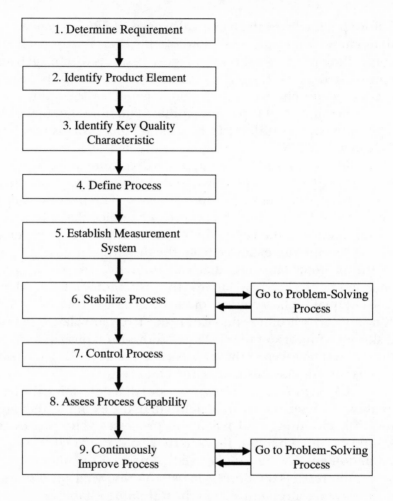

activities" (Cantello, Chalmers, and Evans, 1990) and involves defining gauging procedures and conducting repeatability and reproducibility studies.

In the disk drive example, the processes that affect imbalance of the disk/motor subassembly are disk mounting and disk balance. The balance gauge is the measurement device, and the repeatability of a single gauge should be determined along with the reproducibility of results across multiple gauges.

Table 6.2. SPC Activities for Disk Drive Examples.

Step	Questions to Ask	Conclusions/Actions
1. Determine requirement	What is the requirement of the product, and how will it be measured by customers and suppliers?	Ability to read and write data consistently, measured by error rate
2. Identify product element	What product element affects the requirement?	Disk/motor subassembly, among others
3. Identify key quality characteristics	What is the key quality characteristic related to the element?	Vibration or "warbling" of the subassembly due to imbalance
4. Define process	What is the process related to the characteristic?	Disk mounting and balancing processes
5. Establish measurement system	Is a measurement system defined, and is it repeatable and reproducible?	Conduct imbalance gauge study and make capable
6. Stabilize process	Is the process stable (free from special causes of variation)? If not, what are the special causes, and how can they be removed?	Run chart imbalance after both disk mounting and balancing; remove special causes, which could include incoming materials quality, by working with suppliers
7. Control process	Is the process under statistical control?	Control chart disk mounting and centering processes
8. Assess process capability	Is the process capable of meeting the requirement?	Study process variation in relation to design tolerances
9. Continuously improve process	How can the process be improved to reduce common cause variation?	Modify disk mounting process or centering machine

SPC Steps 6–8. Process stability, or the existence of special causes of variation, must be determined. A simple "run chart" can be used to document process performance and identify major special causes. If special causes are present, they should be studied and sources of unwanted variation eliminated. Any positive sources of variation that may exist should be understood and incorporated into the process. The removal of unwanted special causes produces a process that is considered under "statistical control." The natural process tolerance can then be determined and defined by control limits. The resulting control chart can be used to monitor the process on an ongoing basis for the absence of special causes.

Process stability in the disk drive example should be assessed using the balance gauge after both the disk mounting and balancing processes. Any special causes of variation, such as inconsistent quality of disks received from suppliers, should be investigated and eliminated. Process limits, or the natural process tolerance, can then be determined, and formal "control charts" can be constructed to monitor the two processes.

SPC Step 9. Once the process is in statistical control, its capability to produce within design tolerances can then be determined. Although a variety of capability indexes can be calculated, the underlying concept is that when the tolerance of the process is larger than the specified tolerance, the process is considered incapable of meeting requirements.

In the event the disk mounting and balance processes are not capable of producing a disk drive with sufficiently little vibration to read and write data consistently, either or both would have to be changed to reduce the common causes of variation.

After explaining the approach outlined in the following sections and walking through an example from work that participants are familiar with, challenge them to identify processes from their own jobs to work on. Have them describe how the nine-step approach would apply to their own processes. Ask participants to complete the first four steps on a work process of their own as a homework assignment, since these steps must be completed before statistical techniques can be taught.

SPC Techniques

SPC techniques are most effectively learned if the task-applied training method is employed and the SPC model is used to structure the training. Teach the skills in the context of working on job-related process problems so participants will learn how to apply what they learn to their jobs. They can learn SPC techniques in the process of applying Steps 5 through 9 to the process they began working on in the previous training session.

SPC Steps 1–5. Participants should have already completed Steps 1 through 4, producing a statement of the requirements, identification of the product element and the key quality characteristic, and a flow chart or other documentation of the process in question. Check to see that the work has been done successfully before moving on.

To address Step 5, begin by teaching concepts related to data gathering and measurement, such as sensitivity, precision, accuracy, standards, stability, and validity. Have participants evaluate the actual measurement methods they currently use against these criteria and determine their effectiveness. Introduce the concepts of gauge repeatability and reproducibility, calibration, and measurement correlation at this point, but provide in-depth instruction on conducting such studies to engineers and others responsible for measurement system control.

SPC Step 6. Once participants are confident of their measurement systems, they are ready to move on to the concept of stability. Stability is easily understood with a knowledge of common and special cause variation, and run charts can be introduced as a simple way to assess the stability of processes. Plotting values in time sequence and applying established rules to judge stability make people familiar with some of the basic disciplines they will use later with control charts. Participants may need a number of sessions to stabilize their processes by identifying the existence of special causes (with run charts), identifying the sources of variation (through problem solving), and developing, implementing, and testing solutions to eliminate those causes (using problem solving and decision making).

SPC Step 7. Begin the discussion of controlling processes and constructing control charts by showing participants how to calculate the bounds of common cause variation, known as "control limits," that are inherent in a stable process. It is a good idea to introduce them to the "central limit theorem" at this point, which states that averages of samples plotted from a common cause system will be normally distributed. When special causes appear, the averages will no longer fall within the control limits—which is why control charts are sensitive to variation. Variation that occurs outside of the control limits is a sign that special causes are probably influencing the process.

Before exploring the different types of control charts and how to construct them, participants need to understand the difference between "variable" and "attribute" data. Variable, or continuous, data result from measuring height, weight, length, diameter, duration, and the like. Attribute data result from observing whether certain characteristics are present, such as cracks, scratches, and other defects. Attributes are counted as conforming or not conforming, on or off, go or no-go. Counting the scratches on a surface is an example of collecting attribute data, whereas measuring the length of the scratches is an example of gathering variable data.

Attribute data have two major limitations. First, they have limited value in helping to understand the causes of defects. Knowing the number of scratches (attribute data) is not nearly as helpful in pinpointing causes as knowing the length, depth, and location of the scratches (variable data). Second, attribute data are frequently used to keep track of defects, such as scratches, after they have been made rather than to measure the variation in the process that causes the scratches to occur. Variable data should be sought whenever possible.

Different types of data require different types of control charts. "Average" and "range" control charts, the most common of which are X *bar* and R charts, are used for variable data. These charts control the variable in question by plotting averages of samples taken from a process (X *bar*) as well as the range (R) of values of the samples. Both charts need to have control limits calculated.

Control charts for plotting attribute data take different forms, depending on what is being measured. A "nonconformity" is a single characteristic of a part, and any part may have a number of nonconformities. Any part that has one or more nonconformities is considered to be "nonconforming" (Griffith, 1989, p. 59). For example, a surface that has one or more scratches (nonconformities) is treated as a nonconforming part. Participants must understand this distinction before they are introduced to the most common charts for plotting attribute data: percentage nonconforming (p chart), number nonconforming (np chart), number of nonconformities (c chart), and number of nonconformities per unit (u chart). Once again, teach the concepts first (what needs to be measured) before teaching the tools (the different types of charts).

Process control also requires interpreting the data accurately and taking the proper actions when out-of-control conditions exist. Otherwise, it is a meaningless data-plotting exercise. Data must be plotted and analyzed continually, and the special causes of variation must be identified whenever a process moves out of statistical control. After identifying the causes of out-of-control conditions, permanent solutions must be put in to prevent their recurrence. The person taking the measurements must also be empowered to respond to problems. The greater the lag between measurement and action, the less effective SPC will be.

SPC Steps 8–9. During these steps, the concept of "process capability" comes into play. Understanding process stability enabled participants to identify and investigate special causes of variation. Understanding process control enabled them to monitor their processes to keep them in statistical control. But because a process is stable and in control does not mean it is capable of consistently producing results that meet requirements. The variation of the process, as defined by its control limits, has to be less than the tolerance specified in the design. Begin the discussion of this concept by having participants draw the specification tolerances for their processes on the control charts they previously constructed. Then they can see the relationship of tolerances to their control limits.

One of two discrepancies may occur. Where the process tolerance is larger than the specified tolerance, the process will have to be changed in Step 9 to reduce common causes of variation. Where the process tolerance is less than specified but the distribution of the data is not centered, the overall process variation may be acceptable. However, the process will have to be adjusted to move the distribution average into alignment with the nominal, or target, value of the specification. Depending on people's job functions, you can go into more or less depth on how to calculate the basic capability index—Cp for centered processes and Cpk for uncentered processes. Most people can get by with an understanding of the basic concepts, but engineers and others with technical responsibility will need to know how to conduct process capability studies.

Business Process and Support Service Improvement

The areas that have been most overlooked in past quality efforts and that therefore hold the highest potential for improvement are business processes and support services. Some of the most significant processes in any organization are those that cut across traditional departmental boundaries. These business processes include such important activities as strategic planning, new-product introduction, accounts payable and receivable, customer support, and component qualification. Support services include purchasing, human resources, facilities, data processing, documentation, payroll, and any number of administrative services. For each of these, people from different functions have to coordinate their activities to achieve the desired business result.

Improving business processes and support services is difficult, since no single person or department has complete responsibility for managing them. Although they have not been given much attention in the past, their improvement is increasingly seen as critical to organizational effectiveness. Jim Harrington's book, *Business Process Improvement* (1991), has helped focus my thinking on these important subjects and is an excellent source of information and guidance for the practitioner.

The process management concepts of prevention, variation, process capability, and methodology are as relevant to business process and support service improvement as they are to SPC. The problem with applying them, however, starts with the fact that white-collar work has not traditionally been thought of in process terms. Consequently, little or no process management discipline has been applied to them in the past. As a result, they are seldom defined or documented, and measurement techniques and performance data are almost entirely absent.

The following BPI model has been specifically designed for use in a white-collar environment. It should be used to structure training, just as the SPC model was used to organize training on SPC techniques. BPI training should also be delivered using the task-applied training method, with participants learning by working on their own processes.

BPI Model

The BPI model shown in Figure 6.2 is similar to the SPC model in many respects. The differences result from taking a less formal, less quantitative approach for BPI. But the concepts of determining requirements, defining the process, assessing process performance and capability, identifying opportunities for improvement, and continuously improving pertain to both models.

BPI training should be delivered as a series of learning/doing sessions, where participants work on improving their own business or support service processes. The first session takes two to four hours and gives them an overview of all the BPI activities, as shown in Table 6.3. Subsequent sessions normally take two to three hours each; they should be scheduled at a pace that allows participants to work through each step of the model with their own work processes.

When introducing the BPI model in the first session, use an example all are familiar with to help them understand how the model works. The following example, involving the quali-

Figure 6.2. Business Process Improvement Model.

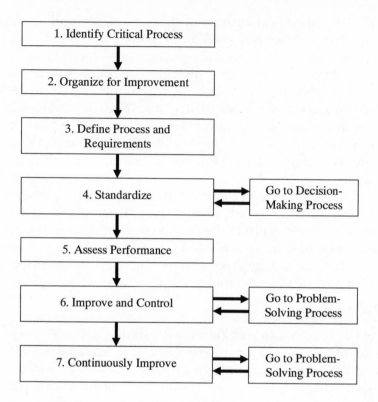

fication of components from suppliers in the electronics industry, illustrates how to apply the model to everyday business situations.

Step 1: Identify the Critical Process. A leading electronics manufacturer determined that it needed to improve its "component qualification" process when a high percentage of components were not listed on the qualified components list (CQL)—as was required before a product could be transferred from preproduction to high-volume production. The process used to qualify components was also called the CQL.

Step 2: Organize for Improvement. The group most affected was the volume production plant, which was being pushed to go

Table 6.3. BPI Activities.

Step	Questions	Activities
1. Identify critical process	Why, specifically, is improvement needed? What process is involved?	Define need for improvement. Identify related business process(es).
2. Organize for improvement	Who are all the people involved and affected? What top manager will support the project? Who should be on the improvement team? Who should take ongoing responsibility?	Identify stakeholders. Identify sponsor for improvement. Form cross-functional BPI team. Appoint process owner.
3. Define process and requirements	Where does the process start and stop? How does it actually work? Who benefits, and what do they need? Who provides inputs, and what is required of them?	Define boundaries. Flow-chart and document. Identify customer requirements, and set standards. Identify suppliers, and define their requirements.
4. Standardize	How should performance be measured? Is the process performed the same way? If not, what is the best way?	Define the measurement system. Evaluate for consistency. Define the best current process and adopt it.
5. Assess performance	How well is the process currently performing? How does it compare to what is needed? What improvements need to be made?	Assess current performance. Compare performance against requirements. Define improvement goals.
6. Improve and control	What steps in the process add no value? How can unnecessary controls and steps be eliminated? Can steps be combined or done an easier way? Can the process be designed to prevent mistakes? How can the process itself be controlled?	Determine the activities that do not add value. Eliminate bureaucracy and other activities that do not add value. Simplify and combine activities. Error-proof the process. Establish in-process measures.
7. Continuously improve	Is performance keeping up with customers' needs? What improvements will be needed in the future? Why should we do things as they have been done in the past?	Solicit feedback and input from customers. Establish improvement goals. Challenge the process and innovate.

into production of new products for which many of the components were not qualified. Bypassing the procedure would not only violate the quality policy but also involve taking the high risks associated with procuring unqualified parts in volume. Responsibility for qualifying components rested with the preproduction materials group, working in conjunction with the component engineering group. The improvement project "sponsor" turned out to be the head of the corporate quality department, and the head of component engineering volunteered to be the "process owner." To be effective, the BPI team needed an influential representative from each of the affected departments, including product development, component engineering, corporate and division quality, division materials, supplier quality engineering, and engineering documentation.

Step 3: Define the Process and Its Requirements. The process started with the product development group, which was responsible for providing specifications for the components, and ended when the component was officially listed on the CQL. Flow charts were developed for the various subprocesses, including component specification, engineering documentation, supplier selection, component qualification, and document processing. The primary internal customer of the process was the volume production plant. The policy stated that all parts must be qualified and listed on the CQL before volume purchasing could be authorized.

Internal suppliers of information and services included product development, component engineering, division quality, division materials, supplier quality engineering, and documentation. The external suppliers were the vendors selected to provide the parts. The component engineering and materials groups required specifications from product development before qualification could begin. The supplier quality engineers also needed the critical quality characteristics of the parts in order to qualify the suppliers' manufacturing processes. The quality and documentation groups needed a complete package of documentation before the component could be listed. And the measurements that would be used to assess process effectiveness were defined as "percent of parts listed on the CQL" and the "cycle time" for each subprocess.

Step 4: Standardize. The flow charts made it obvious that not only were different types of components being qualified differently but the qualification of similar parts was being handled differently by individual engineers. The engineers promptly established two standardized procedures for qualifying electrical and mechanical parts.

Step 5: Assess Performance. It was difficult to assess the historical performance of the process because rigorous measurements were not previously kept. For instance, the documentation group only started timing their process when they received a complete document package, but engineering started their clock as soon as they submitted the package—complete or not. So a new set of measurement procedures had to be agreed to by all parties. The common qualification and measurement procedures allowed new insights on where the real delays were. Some components lacked specifications. Others were backlogged in component engineering because of the heavy work load and the lack of adequate testing facilities. Although the documentation group had generally been blamed for processing delays in the past, they were found to be turning the packages around quickly when they were received complete. The initial improvements, therefore, had to be made by the engineering groups.

Step 6: Improve and Control. New flow charts of the standardized processes, coupled with more accurate measurements, helped identify several opportunities for streamlining the process and reducing bureaucracy. The most obvious one was the large number of approvals required at each step. Signatures of managers who had little knowledge of specific components, and who were frequently unavailable, were needlessly required—delaying the process considerably. The number of signatures was reduced to the minimum needed to ensure process integrity, and substitute managers were identified to fill in when people were out of town. Another easy improvement was consolidating the redundant testing done by different groups.

Other areas were more difficult to fix, such as developing definitive specifications for certain integrated circuits. The policy was amended to allow production to proceed while engineering completed its specification work for certain parts for limited durations. Each subprocess was systematically measured for completeness and cycle time, and a simple report was sent monthly to the head of component engineering. Unusual changes were regularly investigated to identify and eliminate special causes of variation.

Step 7: Continuously Improve. Although the effectiveness and efficiency of the overall CQL process were substantially increased, improvement needed to continue to keep pace with the constantly shrinking "market window" for introducing new products. Products that once took a year or more to get to market were requiring introduction in a matter of months. Pressure from the marketplace was forcing continual reductions of 20 percent or more per year in the cycle time for component qualification. The BPI team also began to explore the idea of involving suppliers much earlier in the product development cycle so the specification and qualification processes could run in parallel instead of in sequence.

The concepts of process management are as simple as they are profound. Taking a prevention-oriented approach to work, understanding the implications of variation, seeing the relationship of process tolerance to design tolerance, and using a structured methodology are fundamental to effective process control and improvement efforts. Help people grasp these concepts first, and then use task-applied training so people can learn the techniques in the context of solving job-related problems. These two approaches are fundamental to successful quality training efforts.

7

Creating a
Learning Organization

FOUR SIMPLE PRINCIPLES
have guided the development of the framework for this book:
use training to facilitate strategy, start simply before getting
complicated, teach people what they need to know when they
need to know it, and teach concepts before techniques. The six-
phase curriculum is structured so that each phase of training
prepares people to take the next step in the strategy; each phase
of training builds on the knowledge and skills developed in the
preceding ones. Phase 1 enables top management to build a
leadership foundation for improvement. Phase 2 builds
everyone's understanding of the organization's strategic direction as well as their personal commitment to carry it out. Phase
3 helps put a quality management system in place to structure
the process, and Phase 4 develops the skills needed to establish
an improvement team infrastructure. With the direction, structure, and team skills in place, Phase 5 gives people the knowledge and skills they need to begin improving the quality of the
organization's processes and support services, the heart of the
entire quality improvement effort.

These five phases provide the basics that every organization needs to begin systematically improving the quality of its
products and services. The final step in the strategy is continuous improvement, and Phase 6 training, which enables im-

provement to be continuous, involves creating a "learning
organization." As *Fortune* magazine recently advised, "Forget
your tired old assumptions about leadership. The most successful corporation of the 1990s will be something called a learning
organization" (Senge, 1990a, p. 4).

Creating a learning organization involves expanding the
capacity of the organization and its people to learn at an ever-
increasing rate. "The ability to learn faster than your competitors," says Arie de Geus (1988) of Royal Dutch/Shell, "may be
the only sustainable competitive advantage." Daniel Kim (1990)
insists that "organizational learning is the root from which all
competitive advantage stems. The level of advantage depends
on the speed and quality of learning, whether behavior change
is accompanied by cognitive change, and whether continual
education is emphasized over sporadic learning. [The learning
organization] consciously manages its learning process to be
consistent with its strategies and objectives through an inquiry-
driven orientation of all its members."

Four methods are discussed in this concluding chapter
to provide insight about how to consciously manage the learning process to help people learn continuously and at increasing
rates.

Integrate All Training

Although people learn best when they can "see the big picture"
and know how the elements fit together, training in most
organizations is highly compartmentalized. For several reasons,
the quality curriculum is normally treated as separate and
distinct from the many other kinds of training, including
management, sales, and operations training. First, the quality
curriculum needs an intense focus to get it started, and keeping
it isolated supports a single-minded focus. Second, it is often
organized under the auspices of the quality department,
whereas training for managers is usually provided by the human resources group, sales training is conducted by the sales
department, and operations training is performed by manufacturing. And third, quality training is often conducted by external consultants rather than internal staff.

In the long term, however, maintaining distinctions between the types of training becomes a barrier to improvement. "I look forward, frankly, to the time when we don't have any quality training as such," says David Kearns. "By then quality should be ingrained into everything we do. Quality shouldn't be a separate piece of training. For example, the training someone gets before going on an assembly line, or the orientation a new person gets, should include quality" (Galagan, 1988).

All training is provided with the same objective in mind: to give people new knowledge and skills that will enable them to perform more effectively and make them more valuable to the organization. Since all training seeks improvement as its goal, it should all be seen as supporting the organization's overall improvement strategy. And many of the skills taught in other curricula are vital to the improvement effort. A few examples follow.

Training to develop managerial skills usually includes such topics as leadership, goal setting, delegation, performance feedback, coaching, interpersonal effectiveness, and meeting management—all of which help managers fulfill their roles in the improvement process (Cocheu, 1992b). Not only is management training central to improvement, but it gains greater relevance and significance for managers when it is taught within the context of improving quality. Instead of reserving this training for managers, it should also be used for developing the skills of team leaders.

Many of the skills taught to salespeople and others in customer contact positions are also very relevant to the improvement process, including building customer partnerships, soliciting customer expectations, listening actively, responding nondefensively to feedback, and negotiating "win-win" solutions. Such training can easily be modified and made appropriate to managers and individual contributors throughout the organization.

The technical, or operations, training provided to people on the factory floor is often conducted separately from training on quality skills. But teaching operations separately from statistical process control (SPC) has resulted in people seeing SPC as a burden added onto what people perceive as their "real" job, which is producing product. The solution is to teach people the process control techniques specific to their operations at the same time they are learning the operations themselves. An example of such an integrated training approach, shown in Figure 7.1, is one that trains people how to "texture" the aluminum substrates of the magnetic disks used in hard disk drives for personal computers. The disk manufacturer used this approach to communicate a clear break with its past philosophy. It had been controlling product quality through inspection by the quality departments; the new approach was to give individual operators personal responsibility for controlling their work processes to prevent defects.

All company training efforts should be examined for opportunities to achieve greater integration and synergy. Realize, however, that this approach requires increased cooperation between departments and a willingness to share resources and expertise. It means putting the company ahead of functional rivalries and working as a team to pursue the common goal of improvement.

Internalize the Ability to Train

Most improvement efforts begin with the advice and guidance of experienced external consultants, who have the perspective of working with a wide variety of organizations. Much of the guidance that consultants provide is in the form of training, since companies often lack internal expertise in the quality disciplines. Although external help is often necessary in the early stages of the improvement effort, it is important for companies to quickly wean themselves from their dependence on outsiders and become more self-sufficient.

There are two alternatives, says Joseph Juran (1992). You can either provide consultants for nonquality professionals or train the "amateurs to become professionals." He feels strongly from his experience over many decades that "training the amateurs to become professionals has outperformed the alternative of providing the planners with consultants" (p. B6).

Figure 7.1. Integrated Texture Operator Training.

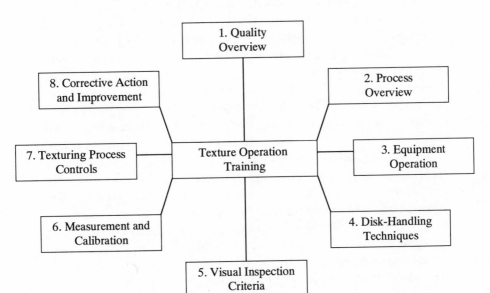

Companies must make the commitment whenever possible to internalize quality expertise and enable employees to train one another. Senge (1990a) describes learning organizations as those "where people continually expand their capacity to create the results they truly desire, where new and expansive patterns of thinking are nurtured, where collective aspiration is set free, and where people are continually learning how to learn together" (p. 3).

Helping people learn how to learn together is essential if learning is to become continuous and if the sporadic, event-driven nature of training in most organizations is to be avoided. Commonly, training is thought of as a specialized activity reserved for the training department and subject matter experts. But in the learning organization, training becomes a company-wide responsibility, shared by everyone at every level. Top managers must teach one another as they expand their own knowledge and insights, as well as train their subordinate managers. In the "waterfall" training approach so popular today, managers are then obligated to turn around and train their people, and so on down through the organization.

The waterfall approach, in which training is conducted successively at each level of the organization, is effective for communicating issues related to company direction. But training and learning must also take place horizontally and spontaneously as people seek to share newfound knowledge with co-workers and colleagues. As Naisbitt and Aburdene (1985) observe, "We are reinventing the corporation from a top-down bureaucracy into a network where everyone learns from everyone else" (p. 78). In an atmosphere where people continuously search for new ideas and eagerly share their latest discoveries with those around them, knowledge can become an organization's only self-renewing and ever-expanding asset.

Internalizing the capability to train means encouraging people's natural desires to learn and talk about what they know. It means expanding traditional job responsibilities to include the obligation to train others. It means giving people time away from their everyday activities to teach others. And it means people have to learn how to organize and communicate their thoughts. "Train-the-trainer" courses must become a central part of the newly integrated curriculum, where everyone learns how to prepare simple instructional materials and develops the public speaking skills needed to present ideas effectively.

Investigate New Methods

Although the first five phases of training provide everyone with the basic improvement skills, more advanced quality tools and techniques are being used by leading companies to help them do everything from improving problem solving and quality planning to designing new products. And new approaches are being developed every day. With the recent explosion in the number of organizations embarking on the quality journey will come a corresponding explosion in the number of new ideas about how to pursue improvement. The following are but four examples of the more sophisticated quality techniques being used today that can help move a company's quality effort to higher levels of attainment.

Hoshin Planning

The two-step approach that was used to build the initial leadership foundation in Phase 1 is a relatively informal process designed to help executives quickly get moving in the right direction. It gives executives the direction they need to determine where they want to go and which path to take to get there.

After the initial planning cycle is complete and it becomes time to begin replanning and goal setting, a more sophisticated technique, known as Hoshin planning, may prove useful. As outlined in Figure 7.2, Hoshin planning is a more formal, highly structured process for planning, executing, and monitoring the improvement process. It seeks to achieve a high level of integration of improvement plans and activities, or the "alignment of targets and means," throughout all levels and functions in the organization (King, 1989).

Given the complexity of Hoshin planning, Bob King of GOAL/QPC believes it must evolve through four stages of organizational learning and maturing (GOAL/QPC Research Committee, 1989a). The first stage of maturity is "management by facts," in which the basic quality tools are used to improve processes. The "self-diagnosis" stage begins when managers are able to diagnose their individual and organizational limitations and take appropriate action. In the "alignment of targets and means" stage, managers begin to align their priorities with one another and work together to achieve a one-year plan. The final stage of implementation is achieved when the planning horizon can effectively be extended to three to five years and the entire organization has become fully involved.

Executives and managers should be introduced to Hoshin planning if there is agreement that a more systematic planning method may be needed. An initial overview seminar can help executives decide whether to pursue Hoshin planning. If the decision is made to proceed, then a team of senior managers needs to be thoroughly trained to lead the implementation. They can serve as internal consultants and as trainers for managers and others, teaching them what they need to know as they move through the process. This approach is

Figure 7.2. Hoshin Planning.

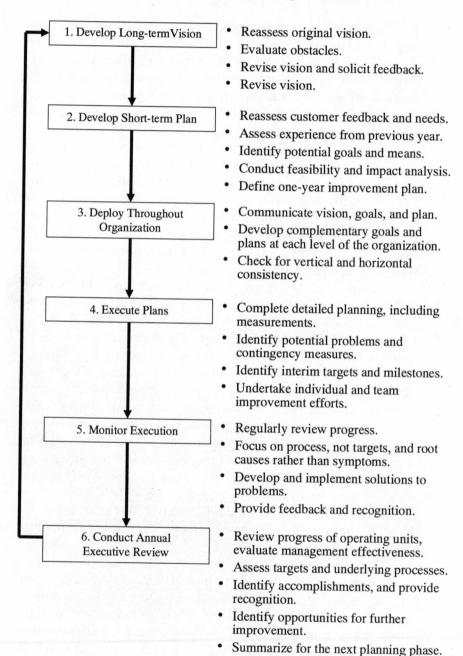

1. Develop Long-term Vision
- Reassess original vision.
- Evaluate obstacles.
- Revise vision and solicit feedback.
- Revise vision.

2. Develop Short-term Plan
- Reassess customer feedback and needs.
- Assess experience from previous year.
- Identify potential goals and means.
- Conduct feasibility and impact analysis.
- Define one-year improvement plan.

3. Deploy Throughout Organization
- Communicate vision, goals, and plan.
- Develop complementary goals and plans at each level of the organization.
- Check for vertical and horizontal consistency.

4. Execute Plans
- Complete detailed planning, including measurements.
- Identify potential problems and contingency measures.
- Identify interim targets and milestones.
- Undertake individual and team improvement efforts.

5. Monitor Execution
- Regularly review progress.
- Focus on process, not targets, and root causes rather than symptoms.
- Develop and implement solutions to problems.
- Provide feedback and recognition.

6. Conduct Annual Executive Review
- Review progress of operating units, evaluate management effectiveness.
- Assess targets and underlying processes.
- Identify accomplishments, and provide recognition.
- Identify opportunities for further improvement.
- Summarize for the next planning phase.

consistent with Juran's belief that "amateurs" should be trained to become professionals in quality planning.

Seven Management Tools

During the early 1970s, the Society of QC Technique Development in Japan began working on a new set of tools for management to use in addressing the demands of the "new era for quality." The society felt that this new era would require extending quality thinking beyond its traditional focus on products and production to every element of the business—indeed, to every aspect of management planning and decision making. What would be needed are tools that "develop the talent of better thinking" (Mizuno, 1988, p. 4).

Before looking at the tools the society developed, it is important to understand the underlying elements, or objectives, of this "better thinking," because they can help show us where we need to expand our own thinking:

> *Conducting multidimensional evaluations:* Looking at problems in their full context and totality, rather than as isolated events
>
> *Eliminating the concept of "recurrence prevention":* Not accepting the belief that failures are inevitable, and finding ways to anticipate and prevent problems from occurring
>
> *Specifying a desirable condition:* Thinking in terms of working toward a more desirable condition, which is more likely to stimulate creativity than talking only about problems
>
> *Making a truly prioritized effort:* Distinguishing the important from the unimportant, and assigning priorities to the steps necessary to improve
>
> *Encouraging systemwide promotion:* Getting the entire organization to work in "organic harmony"; understanding the unspoken "underlying presumptions" in directives; learning how to relate to other departments rather than working in isolation; and getting others to want to cooperate

Actively making changes: Challenging assumptions and avoiding becoming entrenched in routines

Anticipating and predicting the future: Being able to anticipate future directions from trends and take action in advance

The seven management tools developed by the society to stimulate better-quality thinking, shown in Table 7.1, are particularly helpful in synthesizing qualitative information. The three basic functions of the tools are identifying problems by organizing diverse forms of data and clarifying complex causal relationships; facilitating the search for appropriate solutions to problems and organizing steps to achieving quality goals; and assisting in planning and controlling implementation. The tools are complementary to the quantitative tools learned in earlier phases of training; they should be used together for more effective problem solving and planning. Since Hoshin planning achieves its power and advantage over traditional planning approaches through the application of these tools, the training for both can effectively be integrated.

Like the earlier tools, these new management tools should be taught when they are needed during team activities, using the task-applied training method. Gitlow (1990) recommends a curriculum of one-day workshops for each tool, using a modular instructional format similar to that shown in Table 5.1. Although seven days of training, even when they are spread over many weeks, may be unrealistic for many organizations, the difficulty of mastering these new tools should not be underestimated. And managers of team members should be encouraged to attend the sessions when participants are making their presentations, to reinforce the integration of these tools into the workplace.

Quality Function Deployment

Who would not like to find a way to get products to market with twice the productivity, half the cost, and twice the quality—and in two-thirds the time? Of course, we all would. These objectives

Table 7.1. New Quality Tools.

Tool	Function	When to Use
Affinity diagram (also called KJ method)	Gathers and organizes diverse types of data, and categorizes them into clusters based on the natural relationships among the items	When the situation is confused and only disordered verbal information is available
Relations diagram	Begins to draw the logical connections brought to the surface in the affinity diagram; starts with a central idea, generates a lot of ideas, and delineates observed patterns	When you need to analyze a problem or situation where complex cause-and-effect relationships exist
Tree diagram (also called systematic method)	Searches out the most appropriate means or methods for achieving a goal; breaks the main subject into elements, and shows relationships	When you need to break a problem or solution into its component parts and understand the relationships between the parts
Matrix diagram	Shows relationships and connections among elements on multiple dimensions	When you need to explore the relationships among sets of data on multiple dimensions
Matrix data analysis	Arranges the data derived from the matrix diagram on two dimensions to graphically show the true strength of relationships between variables; analyzes data numerically, unlike the other tools	When you believe a relationship exists and you need to see the strength of the relationship (and numerical data exist)
Process decision program chart	Maps out possible events, anticipates outcomes, and prepares contingency actions that will lead to the best possible solution	When the consequences of error are high and you need to prevent or minimize the impact of undesired outcomes
Arrow diagram	Develops a network diagram of activities and milestones for implementation planning; is closely associated with PERT and CPM planning methods	When you are developing a plan and the sequence and duration of activities are known; when you need to see the relationship among plan elements in time

are attainable with the aid of quality function deployment (QFD), insist William Eureka and Nancy Ryan (1988) of the American Supplier Institute. QFD is a systematic method for translating the "voice of the customer" into company requirements at each stage of the product development cycle, from marketing to production. Although not conceptually different from the way many companies currently strive to turn customers' requirements into marketable products, QFD provides a systematic way to define those requirements and deploy them throughout the organization.

The QFD process, summarized in Figure 7.3, starts with product planning, in which marketing works with customers to define their requirements and engineering works with marketing to determine a design that will satisfy them. The initial QFD "matrix diagram" shows the relationship between customer requirements and the corresponding design requirements. A matrix diagram can also be used to clarify the relationships among the various engineering requirements themselves, which may complement or conflict with each other, and to tie in competitive assessments.

Consider an example. Car buyers want doors that are easy to open and close and that also stay open when the car is on a hill (customer requirements). The corresponding design requirements, minimizing the force it takes to close the door on level ground and maintaining sufficient resistance so it remains open on a slope, must both be met even though they conflict. These are the kinds of relationships the QFD quality matrix can make explicit. (This discussion draws on the works of Hauser and Clausing, 1988; Bersbach and Wahl, 1991; and ReVelle, 1991.)

In the next step, product design, engineering turns the design requirements into part characteristics. In our car example, the weight of the door and the characteristics of the hinge and spring mechanisms would have to be specified to meet the design and customer requirements. Engineering then works with manufacturing in the process planning step to relate part characteristics to manufacturing operations, which would include the machinery required to produce the parts.

Figure 7.3. Quality Function Deployment (QFD).

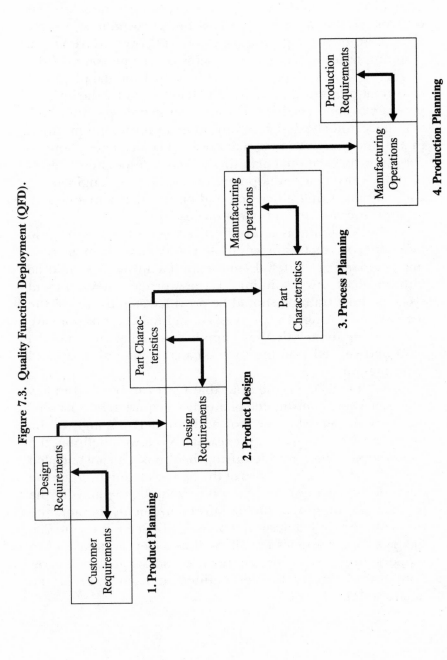

During production planning, manufacturing operations are used to derive production requirements, including process controls for the machinery and assembly procedures.

One of the big advantages of QFD over conventional planning approaches is that it helps overcome some of the largest barriers to improvement: interdepartmental planning, coordination, and communication. It helps reduce the interdepartmental conflicts that can arise if marketing specifies products that cannot be designed and engineering designs products that cannot be easily manufactured. QFD facilitates cooperative interorganizational planning, which is desperately needed to reduce product development cycles, increase engineering and manufacturing efficiency, and ensure that everyone's efforts are focused on customers' needs.

QFD training is most effectively conducted with cross-functional product teams composed of members from marketing, engineering, materials, and manufacturing. It should be introduced at the beginning of a new-product development cycle, and the training should be provided step by step as the team moves through the process. Far-sighted organizations are also working to include their suppliers as well as customers in QFD and related training to maximize communication and coordination.

It should be pointed out that QFD can be used in any situation where coordinated planning is required. Its versatility becomes obvious when we look at the underlying logic of the QFD matrix diagram. The process starts out with defining the "whats" (ends) and then identifying the "hows" (means) needed to satisfy the whats. The hows of the first level then become the whats of the next level down; in the example, the hows of the product planning step, the design requirements, became the whats of the product design step. As can be seen in Figure 7.4, this same logic applies equally well as a deployment tool to support Hoshin planning, where the corporate goals and plans flow down and are further defined at each level of the organization.

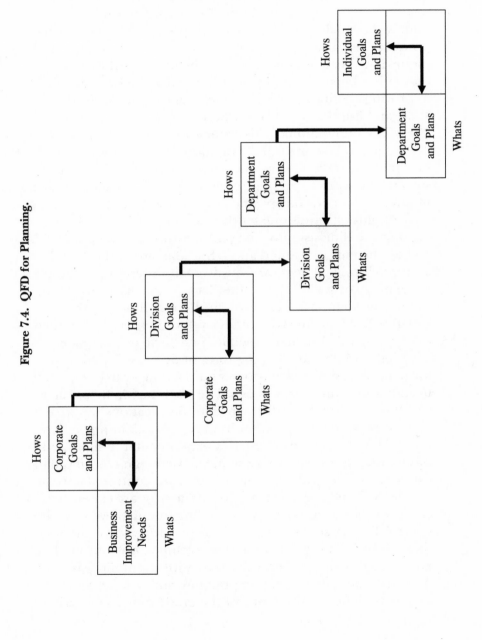

Figure 7.4. QFD for Planning.

Taguchi Methods

Dr. Genichi Taguchi, a Japanese quality engineer, brought several innovations to traditional experimental design techniques that make his methods very powerful for improving products and processes. As important as his statistical techniques have been, however, perhaps his most significant contribution has been the conceptual framework he developed for improving quality. (This discussion draws on the works of Ross, 1988, and Eureka and Ryan, 1988.)

The foundation of this framework is the concept known as the "quality loss function." Traditional quality control theory says that a product, part, or service is acceptable if it falls somewhere within specified tolerances. For instance, a part may have a dimension specification of one inch, with a tolerance of plus or minus one-tenth of an inch (1 inch ± .1 inch). As long the dimension of the part lies within .9 inch and 1.1 inches, the part is deemed good. But what about the part that is .89 inch or 1.11 inches? Can .01-inch difference magically make one part good and another bad? Taguchi says it cannot. Rather, he demonstrates through the loss function that any variation from the ideal or nominal value, even within specified tolerances, will ultimately result in some form of loss to society. That loss—which can take the form of decreased quality, performance, reliability, or customer satisfaction—can be equated to additional, unnecessary costs. The loss function helps clarify why the traditional "conformance to specifications" approach must be replaced by a philosophy of continuous improvement.

The objective of Taguchi's experimental design methods is to achieve a "robust" design. Such a design is achieved in two steps: (1) identifying which factors are controllable (control factors) and which are not controllable or are expensive to control (noise factors); and (2) finding optimal levels for the control factors so that the highest performance is attained despite the presence of noise. For example, one automobile engine is designed to be used only with premium gasoline. Another is designed to run on premium and regular. Since the engine designer cannot control the grade of gasoline drivers will use (noise factor), an engine that can accommodate any grade of fuel is a more robust design than the other and will cause fewer problems for car owners.

Achieving a robust design, therefore, requires an understanding of the environmental conditions in which a product will be used and of the ways a product will be applied by the user. It is here that the power of combining quality techniques can be realized. QFD identifies the customers' requirements, such as "use with all grades of fuel," and defines design requirements to satisfy them. Taguchi methods can then be applied to evaluate how to design products that will perform satisfactorily under a wide variety of conditions and applications. The control factors that are critical to product performance, identified through Taguchi methods, can then become the subject of statistical process control techniques in the factory.

Training in Taguchi methods is typically reserved for engineering and quality assurance personnel and is best conducted with the task-applied training approach, in which participants have real projects to work on and learn the methods in the process of applying them. Unfortunately, this approach is frequently not possible, since the training is often available only through public seminars. When this is the only option, make sure the training is provided just in time by having participants and their managers identify improvement projects prior to attending. Knowledge of this complex subject dissipates quickly and must be applied immediately. If possible, it is better to contract with the external instructor to conduct the seminar in-house and take the time to customize the training with company-specific examples. The instructor should also be retained to provide postseminar consulting, to guide participants through their initial applications of the techniques and help them build skills they can apply to other projects in the future.

Although the statistical techniques are of most value to engineers, the conceptual framework that Taguchi provides is equally valuable to managers and nontechnical individual contributors. It provides a much deeper insight into the concepts of variation, prevention, poor quality costs, and cause and effect, which can help make everyone's improvement efforts more effective. When it is difficult for managers to understand what continuous improvement really means, why it is important, and how it differs from mere conformance to specifications, exposure to the loss function can be very enlightening (Cocheu, 1992c). Similarly, Taguchi methods provide a tangible example of what it means to take the big step from fire fighting and problem solving to prevention. Anticipating uncontrolled factors and designing products and processes to minimize their potential negative impact on the customer is a much surer path toward quality than reacting to problems and performing damage control after they occur.

Develop a Learning Strategy

If the rate at which an organization and its people learn is becoming its only sustainable source of competitive advantage, then we need to change the way we think about learning. Companies can ill afford to leave learning to chance; it must become a conscious, explicit activity that is planned and managed. Just as organizations need an improvement strategy, so do they need a strategy for continuous, accelerated learning. A discussion of five elements of such a strategy follows.

Learning from Experience

Experience is obviously the greatest teacher of all. We learn to do most things by trial and error—taking some action, observing the consequences, and modifying our action as a result. We learn what works and does not work, what gets rewarded and what does not, and what to do again and what to avoid doing— all by trial and error. But we can greatly accelerate our learning by turning our everyday experience from a haphazard series of apparently unrelated events into a learning laboratory. The way to start is by looking at the improvement process as a series of learning opportunities. As Blaauw and During of the Netherlands stress, "the process of setting quality objectives, working to meet the objectives, checking the results and comparing them to the objectives, taking corrective action and learning must go on forever" (1990).

Problem solving can also be a great teacher if the root causes of problems are sought, rather than their symptoms, and if the findings are generalized and communicated to others. Banging on my television set when the picture is bad may solve the problem temporarily, but I do not learn much from this "solution." If I find the root cause of the picture problem and develop a broader understanding of how the television works that can be applied to other situations, then the value of the knowledge I have gained is greater than the solution to the immediate problem. If I then take the time to communicate my newfound knowledge to family or friends, then I have multiplied the value and impact of my learning many times.

Learning from experience means learning from our mistakes as well as our successes. It means taking action and reflecting on the results. The heart of Shewhart's "plan, do, check, act" cycle, for example, is a reflective, experiential learning process (Deming, 1982, p. 88). Learning occurs when a person is able to assess a problem or situation, develop a solution or hypothesis about probable remedies, take action, see what happens, and make adjustments based on the results. Learning organizations understand that process and provide an environment in which people can take risks, make mistakes, and learn from them. A story has circulated as part of the folklore of how a major company dealt with an executive who made a very costly mistake and got called into the president's office. As he walked nervously into the office, he blurted out: "I guess you called me in to fire me." Whereupon the president responded, "Don't be silly—I wouldn't fire you after spending so much money on your education."

Question Assumptions

Although experience is often the best teacher, it can also become a major limitation when one is confronted with new and different circumstances. What worked in an apparently similar situation in the past may not be appropriate now. The illusion that the future is simply a linear extension of the past and that yesterday's solutions are adequate for today can be a blindfold that keeps us from seeing new and different approaches. Keeping our eyes open starts by questioning our hidden assumptions, those beliefs that underlie all our thinking and decisions and are seldom explicitly thought about or discussed. In attempting to effect a paradigm shift, or to foster the ability to think beyond the constraints of experience, learning organizations must be able to shine the light of inquiry on those values, beliefs, and assumptions that unknowingly shape our everyday thinking.

Developing an empowered work force, as an example, means overcoming past experiences that lead people to believe they must wait for direction from above to know what to do. It also means managers overcoming the traditional misconceptions that they have to know everything and make all the decisions. It is up to top management to begin creating an environment for people where it is safe to take risks and question each other's assumptions in an effort to seek creative solutions and struggle against the limitations of our current thinking.

Learn from Others

One of the major accomplishments of the recent quality movement has been to make sharing and learning from others not only acceptable but fashionable. The now popular practice of "benchmarking" enables companies to look beyond themselves and seek out the experiences of other organizations that excel in areas of particular interest. According to the *1992 Award Criteria* for the Baldrige Award, "benchmarks may also serve a useful purpose in stimulating breakthrough thinking. Benchmarks offer the opportunity to achieve significant improvements based on adoption and adaptation. . . . They help encourage creativity through exposure to alternative approaches and results, . . . thus encouraging major improvements rather than only incremental refinements of existing approaches" (National Institute of Standards and Technology, 1991, p. 8).

Companies interested in improving their distribution activities, for example, flock to L. L. Bean and Federal Express, both of which are known for efficiently managing distribution with high levels of performance and customer satisfaction. Those interested in understanding effective quality planning frequently visit Hewlett-Packard, which has worked hard for several years to implement Hoshin planning in its Japanese and American facilities. Understanding what is possible by observing world-class organizations can help develop the creative tension needed to move people beyond the comfort of the status quo.

Learning organizations work to eradicate the "not-invented-here syndrome" and seek to learn from industry leaders. And they weave benchmarking into the fabric of their planning processes by teaching people the necessary disciplines and giving them the time required to do it.

Learn with Other Professionals

Professional organizations—such as the American Society for Quality Control, the Association for Quality and Participation, and the American Society for Training and Development—can provide a wide variety of learning resources and opportunities. In addition to publishing monthly journals with topical articles, they publish extensive lists of the most current books and training materials on subjects ranging from training methods and quality circles to reliability engineering. The investments that companies make in libraries of learning resources pay for themselves many times as people begin to actively seek knowledge and apply what they learn.

Associations also encourage people to learn from one another through monthly meetings of local chapters and national and regional conventions. Such meetings provide chances for people to meet their counterparts from other companies and industries to discuss subjects of mutual interest and develop informal networks for sharing and communication.

Seminars on the full spectrum of quality subjects are readily available through associations, universities, community colleges, and consulting firms.

Enthusiastic learners also grow in their professions by serving on committees and taking other volunteer roles within the associations of their choice. Paying the annual dues for membership in the appropriate professional organizations is an excellent investment for any company working to transform itself into a learning organization.

Make Learning a Job Responsibility

The learning organization becomes a reality when learning is elevated to the status of a job responsibility—a duty, like others, that is included in people's job descriptions, objectives, and performance appraisals. Imagine a time when merely doing your job is not enough, when continuous learning becomes a management expectation and condition of employment. Imagine a time when learning moves beyond the realm of simple "job training" and "personal development" to become a key competitive strategy. When learning is seen as a job responsibility, rather than nonproductive time away from work, people will be able to experience themselves as the naturally inquisitive learners we are. "Learning organizations are possible because, deep down, we are all learners. No one has to teach an infant to learn. . . . They are intrinsically inquisitive, masterful learners who learn to walk, speak, and pretty much run their households on their own. Learning organizations are possible because not only is it our nature to learn but we love to learn" (Senge, 1990a, p. 3).

A Beacon in the Storm

On the new frontier of quality, those with vision must discover ways to help their organizations evolve into safe havens for lifelong learning and continuous improvement. Evolution takes place over time, and the results cannot be predicted. Although we have much to learn about how to make the transition successfully, one thing is certain: the most stubborn obstacle to learning and improvement we face today is the prevalence of fear in organizational life. It is particularly insidious because, while it cannot even be discussed in public, it saps people's enthusiasm, commitment, and creativity—the lifeblood of improvement.

Deming made "Drive out fear" the eighth of his fourteen "principles for transformation of Western management." "No one can put in his best performance unless he feels secure. *Se* comes from the Latin, meaning without, and *cure* means fear or care. *Secure* means without fear, not afraid to express ideas, not afraid to ask questions. Fear takes on many faces. A common denominator of fear in any form, anywhere, is loss from impaired performance and padded figures" (p. 59).

Schaffer and Thompson (1992) say the improvement "efforts of many companies have as much impact on operational and financial results as a ceremonial rain dance has on the weather." Their conclusion is that companies have confused the means and the ends, making too many preparatory investments and devoting excessive time to ephemeral quality activities without focusing on how best to obtain meaningful, bottom-line results.

Although their observation is valid, I would say the preoccupation with activities that do not really improve organizations is a symptom of the problem. The root cause is fear—fear of saying what needs to be said, fear of challenging strongly held beliefs and assumptions, fear of sticking one's neck out to do what is best for customers and for the organization, and the ultimate fear that being true to oneself is not really acceptable in business.

There is much to do to improve as rapidly as the world demands, and many feel they have to make up for lost time—create a vision, pound out a strategy, communicate and train, listen to customers, form partnerships with suppliers, set goals, form teams, improve processes, and so on. The "to do" list is long and intimidating, and checking off all the items still will not ensure success. Trying to keep all the balls in the air at once can be an overwhelming juggling act, even for an experienced hand.

The strategy and the training curriculum presented here are intended to guide you down the path of improvement.

Ultimately, however, there is no secret formula, no approach that is right for all organizations at all times. For better or worse, improvement is dependent on people and is just about as predictable. Assess where your organization is along the path, and identify what you have done well and can build on and what areas have been overlooked and need greater attention.

But when you begin to feel overwhelmed and lost at sea, focus on the one beacon of light that can help you keep a steady course: driving fear out of your organization is the single most important thing you can do. Helping people feel secure and unafraid to say and do what they know to be right more than compensates for an incomplete strategy or an inadequate training curriculum. Improvement is not so much a question of motivating people as it is one of liberating their natural enthusiasm from the grip of fear.

RESOURCE

Five Influential Quality Philosophies: Deming, Juran, Feigenbaum, Crosby, and Imai

Organizations often make one of two mistakes regarding quality philosophy and the related training. One is to overemphasize it and naively believe that it will, by itself, bring about improvement. As W. Edwards Deming (1982) warns, "An important obstacle is the supposition that improvement of quality and productivity is accomplished suddenly by affirmation of faith" (p. 126). In the 1980s, this mistake was made by numerous companies that relied on training from well-known quality experts.

The other mistake is to gloss over the "philosophy" training in a rush to get to the more practical, tangible skills, such as statistical process control. Organizations want to quickly start controlling work processes and improving their products and services. The problem with this approach is that people are not given an understanding of how statistics and other quality techniques fit into the "bigger picture." And they are more than a little skeptical about management's commitment to improvement.

Neither approach, overemphasizing or underemphasizing "awareness" training, gives people the grounding they need to make significant, continuous improvement. Daniel Kim's comments, quoted in Chapter One, are particularly pertinent here: "TQ [total quality] is both an all-encompassing

173

philosophy about the whole enterprise of running the business and a set of statistical tools. . . . Without this philosophy, TQ is reduced to a bag of tools. . . . Without the statistical tools, TQ is nothing more than a guiding light to a goal that offers no help for navigating the terrain. TQ's success lay in linking the lofty goals for top management with a set of tools to achieve these goals" (1990).

The six-phase training approach described in Chapters Two through Seven enables organizations to avoid these mistakes. It provides the necessary balance between philosophy (in Phases 1 and 2) and systems, techniques, and tools (in Phases 3 through 6). But a solid understanding of quality requires at least passing familiarity with the philosophies of a small group of quality experts whose pioneering works have paved the way for all who follow. Included here are overviews of W. Edwards Deming, Joseph M. Juran, Armand V. Feigenbaum, and Philip B. Crosby, as well as a relative newcomer, Masaaki Imai. Skimming the surface of each guru's thinking will help you articulate a quality philosophy that is consistent with the values of your organization.

W. Edwards Deming

Dr. Deming is famous for introducing statistical quality control to post–World War II Japan, starting with a seminar sponsored by the Japanese Union of Scientists and Engineers in 1950. Deming has probably done more than anyone to help us understand variation and its impact on quality. Although best known in the West as a statistician, his advocacy of statistical techniques is grounded in his much broader understanding of business and economics. Deming's philosophy of improvement, documented in *Out of the Crisis* (1982), includes his fourteen "principles for transformation of Western management":

1. Create constancy of purpose toward improvement of product and service, with the aim to become competitive, stay in business, and provide jobs.

2. Management must adopt the new philosophy, awaken to the challenge, learn its responsibilities, and provide leadership for change.
3. Cease dependence on inspection to achieve quality by building quality into the product in the first place.
4. End the practice of awarding business on the basis of price tag alone. Instead, minimize total cost. Move toward a single supplier for any one item through a long-term relationship of loyalty and trust.
5. Improve constantly and forever the system of production and service, to improve quality and productivity, and constantly decrease costs.
6. Institute training on the job.
7. Institute leadership. The aim of supervision should be to help people and machines to do a better job.
8. Drive out fear, so that everyone may work effectively for the company.
9. Break down barriers between departments. People in research, design, sales, and production must work as a team to foresee problems that may be encountered with the product or service.
10. Eliminate slogans, exhortations, and targets for the work force which ask for zero defects and new levels of productivity. Such exhortations only create adversarial relationships, since the bulk of the causes of low quality and productivity belong to the system and lie beyond the power of the work force to remedy.
11. Eliminate work standards (quotas) on the factory floor and substitute leadership.
12. Remove barriers that rob the worker of the right to pride of workmanship. This means

the abolishment of the annual merit rating and management by objectives.

13. Institute a vigorous program of education and self-improvement.
14. Put everybody in the company to work to accomplish the transformation—it is everybody's job [pp. 23–24].

More recently, Deming has articulated a system of "profound knowledge" that underlies his theory of management and provides the basis for understanding his fourteen points. This system includes the following areas:

1. Nature of variation
2. Losses due to tampering (making changes without knowledge of special and common causes of variation)
3. Minimizing the risk from the above two (through the use of control charts)
4. Interaction of forces, dependence and interdependence
5. Losses from management decisions made in the absence of knowledge of variation
6. Losses from the successive application of random forces that may be individually unimportant (such as workers training other workers)
7. Losses from competition for market share and trade barriers
8. Theory of extreme values
9. Statistical theory of failure
10. Theory of knowledge in general
11. Psychology, including intrinsic and extrinsic motivation
12. Learning theory
13. Need for the transformation to leadership from grading and ranking
14. Psychology of change (Gitlow, 1990, pp. 25–26)

More than any of the other quality gurus, Deming takes a systems view of quality and management, as illustrated by his application of the statistical concepts of special and common causes of variation to management practices. For example, Deming insists on abolishing annual merit ratings of employees because he believes the "apparent differences between people arise almost entirely from action of the system that they work in, not from the people themselves" (p. 110). In other words, he insists that managers mistakenly confuse common causes of variation in performance (the system in which people work) with special causes (the actions of people themselves).

His many early contributions to our understanding of quality management include popularizing the following important concepts: common (random) and special (nonrandom) causes of variation; the quality "chain reaction" (increasing quality increases productivity, which lowers costs and helps capture market share); "production viewed as a system" that includes customers and suppliers; "operational definitions" (which put communicable meaning into concepts); and his application of the Shewhart "plan-do-check-act" cycle of continuous improvement.

Joseph M. Juran

According to Kaoru Ishikawa, the early teachings of Deming resulted in an overemphasis on statistical quality control in Japan. "There is a limit to statistical quality control which has engineers as its prime movers. The Juran visit [to Japan in 1954] created an atmosphere in which QC [quality control] was regarded as a tool of management, thus creating an opening for the establishment of total quality control as we know it today" (1985, p. 19). Like Deming, Juran too began as a statistician, but he quickly eschewed a rigid statistical approach. He takes a consumer-oriented approach to defining quality, saying it is determined by a product's "fitness for use." Juran has defined five major dimensions that make up fitness for use: quality of design, quality of conformance, availability, safety, and field use (March, 1990). Most recently, Juran has insisted, in concert with Deming, that "evaluation of end product [and service] quality is now based on response to *customer needs* rather than on conformance to specifications" (1992, p. B2).

In his desire to communicate effectively with financially oriented executives, Juran became a strong advocate of the "cost-of-quality" approach to determining quality goals. The four components of the cost-of-quality model are the costs associated with appraisal (efforts to find errors, such as inspection), prevention (efforts to avoid errors, such as training), internal failures (errors discovered prior to shipment, such as scrap and rework), and external failures (errors discovered after shipment, including warranty and repair costs). Quality goals should, therefore, be aimed at minimizing the costs of quality, which is done by continuing to improve quality until there is no longer a positive economic return. The idea of quality optimization, hotly contested these days by most quality theorists and practitioners, implies that "zero defects" is not a practical goal; spending on prevention and appraisal should continue only until no longer justified by commensurate savings in internal and external failures.

Juran got a lot of attention in the early 1960s with his advocacy of finding significant breakthrough opportunities caused by "chronic problems." These opportunities are greatest in the early stages of an organization's quality efforts, when its failure costs greatly exceed its costs of prevention and appraisal. Juran's breakthrough sequence has seven steps:

1. Break through attitudes.
2. Identify the vital few projects.
3. Organize for breakthrough.
4. Conduct the analysis.
5. Determine how to overcome resistance to change.
6. Institute change.
7. Institute controls (1964, pp. 15–17).

More recently, Juran (1986) has emphasized his Quality Trilogy (a registered trademark) for managing improvement projects, which describes the planning, control, and improvement processes:

1. Quality planning
   a. Identify customers, both internal and external.

    b. Determine customer needs.

    c. Develop features for goods and services that respond to customer needs.

    d. Establish quality goals that, at minimum cost, meet the needs of customers and suppliers alike.

    e. Develop processes that meet the quality goals under operating conditions.

2. Quality control

    a. Choose subjects to control.

    b. Choose units of measurement.

    c. Establish measurement.

    d. Establish standards of measurement.

    e. Establish standards of performance.

    f. Measure actual performance.

    g. Interpret actual performance versus the standard.

    h. Take action on the difference.

3. Quality improvement

    a. Demonstrate the need for improvement.

    b. Identify specific projects for improvement.

    c. Organize to guide the projects.

    d. Organize for diagnosis.

    e. Diagnose to find causes.

    f. Provide remedies.

    g. Prove that the remedies work under operating conditions.

    h. Provide control to hold the gain.

Armand V. Feigenbaum

Although not as well known as Deming and Juran, Feigenbaum has had extensive influence on the evolution of quality management. With the publication of his seminal work, *Total Quality Control* (1983), he changed quality from being the sole responsibility of a small group of technical specialists to being the mutual responsibility of all functions in the pursuit of customer satisfaction. According to Feigenbaum, "total quality control

(TQC) is an effective system for integrating the quality development, quality maintenance, and quality improvement efforts of the various groups in an organization so as to enable marketing, engineering, production, and service at the most economical levels which allow for customer satisfaction" (p. 6).

The underlying philosophy of his total quality view is that "quality is a customer determination, not an engineer's determination, not a marketing determination or a general management determination. It is based upon the customer's actual experience with the product or service, measured against his or her requirements—stated or unstated, conscious or merely sensed, technically operational or entirely subjective—and always representing a moving target in a competitive market" (p. 7). He goes on to say, "Product and service quality can be defined as: The total composite product and service characteristics of marketing, engineering, manufacture, and maintenance through which the product and service in use will meet the expectations of the customer." More thoroughly than the others, Feigenbaum has defined the total quality system in which every function in the organization bears responsibility for satisfying the customer.

Interestingly, Ishikawa takes issue with Feigenbaum on this very point and feels that Feigenbaum's approach to TQC still places too much emphasis on the traditional quality control department. Fearing quality could become no one's job if it were everybody's job (Ishikawa, 1985), Feigenbaum advocated that "TQC be buttressed and serviced by a well organized management function whose only area of specialization is product quality" (p. 90). Ishikawa argues that Feigenbaum's Western-type professionalism led him to advocate that TQC be conducted essentially by quality specialists. But the Japanese approach differs from Feigenbaum's original TQC concept: "Since 1949 we have insisted on having all divisions and all employees become involved in studying and promoting QC. Our movement has never been the exclusive domain of QC specialists" (Ishikawa, 1985, p. 90). To differentiate the Japanese approach from Feigenbaum's TQC, Ishikawa explains, the term "company-wide quality control" is used.

Philip Crosby

Crosby probably did more than any other individual to popularize quality in the United States during the late 1970s and early 1980s, with his now classic *Quality Is Free: The Art of Making Quality Certain* (1979). Crosby is a master of coining memorable phases; "zero defects" and "Do it right the first time" captured the imagination of many U.S. executives searching for a simple-to-understand quality philosophy.

Crosby (1984) preaches a simple formula of "four absolutes" that make it possible for everyone to understand quality the same way and overcome the "conventional wisdom" about quality: (1) the definition of quality is conformance to requirements, not goodness; (2) the system of quality is prevention, not appraisal; (3) the only performance standard is zero defects, not "That's close enough"; and (4) the measurement of quality is the price of nonconformance, not indexes (pp. 64-68).

The four absolutes provide the foundation for Crosby's quality philosophy, and his "fourteen steps of quality improvement" provide the road map for implementing his program:

1. *Management commitment:* Having management demonstrate where it stands on quality
2. *Quality improvement team:* Organizing to run the improvement program
3. *Quality measurement:* Determining and communicating opportunities for quality improvement
4. *Cost of quality:* Setting up a cost-of-quality system
5. *Quality awareness:* Having everyone in the organization become more concerned about the conformance of the product and the quality reputation of the organization
6. *Corrective action:* Providing a method to resolve problems forever
7. *Zero defects planning:* Preparing for the formal launch of a quality improvement program
8. *Employee education:* Enabling people to carry out their responsibilities in the quality program

9. *Zero defects day:* Creating an event to highlight quality and quality accomplishments to all employees

10. *Goal setting:* Having supervisors establish quality improvement goals with their people

11. *Error cause removal:* Providing employees a method of communicating problems to management

12. *Recognition:* Providing recognition for progress and achievements

13. *Quality councils:* Bringing together the organization's quality people to communicate regularly

14. *Do it all over again:* Emphasizing that quality improvement is a never-ending cycle (pp. 99–120)

Masaaki Imai

Imai, author of the popular book *Kaizen: The Key to Japan's Success* (1986), is a relative newcomer to the group of quality luminaries. He believes that focusing on issues like quality or productivity promotes piecemeal solutions and ignores the thread that ties everything together: *kaizen,* the philosophy of continuous improvement. In trying to understand Japan's postwar "economic miracle," Imai comments, Westerners studied such factors as total quality control, quality circles, suggestions systems, just-in-time inventory systems, automation, and unique management practices (including lifetime employment and seniority-based wages). Yet, he feels, they failed to grasp the simple truth that lies behind the many myths concerning Japanese success: "The implication of TQC in Japan has been that these concepts have helped Japanese companies generate a process-oriented way of thinking and develop strategies that assure continuous improvement involving people at all levels of the organizational hierarchy. The message of the KAIZEN strategy is that not a day should go by without some kind of improvement being made somewhere in the company. The belief that there should be unending improvement is deeply ingrained" (p. 4).

Imai believes that the challenge to the West is to change

"innovation- and results-oriented" thinking (R criteria) to also incorporate process-oriented thinking (P criteria): "KAIZEN generates process-oriented thinking, since processes must be improved before we get improved results. . . . In other words, the process is considered just as important as the obviously intended results" (pp. 16–17). It is a belief that improvement for its own sake is the surest way to strengthen a company's overall competitiveness. Creating a cooperative atmosphere and corporate culture has been an inseparable part of *kaizen* programs. But such an achievement necessitates the following:

- Constant efforts to improve industrial relations
- Emphasis on training and education
- Development of informal leadership among workers
- Formation of small-group improvement activities
- Support and recognition of workers' *kaizen* efforts (P criteria)
- Conscious efforts to make work a place where workers can pursue life goals
- Bringing social life into the workshop as much as practical
- Training for supervisors so they can communicate better and relate more positively with workers
- Discipline (in terms of following procedures) in the workshop

Summary

This discussion of the thinking of the quality experts may have raised as many questions as it has answered. Do significant differences between them exist, or are the differences largely semantic? Tom Peters (1988) has asked, "Which system? There's a lot of confusion here. Should you follow W. Edwards Deming, father of the Japanese quality revolution . . . ? Or Phil Crosby, author of *Quality Is Free* . . . ? Or Armand Feigenbaum's *Total Quality Control*? Or Joseph Juran? Or invent a system of your own?" His conclusion: "Frankly, it makes little difference which you choose, among the top half-dozen or so, as long as it is thorough and followed rigorously" (p. 74).

Certainly there are many areas of commonality among the experts. All believe that quality is ultimately defined by the customer. All would say that executive understanding and commitment are the cornerstone of improvement. All advocate extensive training and believe that employee involvement is a prerequisite to progress. And all insist that instituting significant changes in corporate priorities and culture is the major challenge facing organizations today. But these similarities among the experts do not deny the importance and value of their differences.

Juran's approach is a very practical and straightforward means of organizing and managing improvement projects. It is difficult to argue with his ideas: there are breakthrough opportunities in our organizations; improvement ultimately happens project by project; and such projects necessarily have planning, control, and improvement phases. Juran's approach appears to be complementary to, rather than incompatible with, the others.

Ishikawa's comments aside, Feigenbaum clearly was on the right track in trying to get all functions in the company to cooperate in the improvement process. Forty years after the first edition of *Total Quality Control,* we are still struggling to "break down the barriers between departments," to get people in sales and engineering to work as a team with the production and quality departments. The barriers to cooperation that remain between the departments in our companies also serve as barriers to quality improvement.

Crosby oversimplifies the subject on purpose. He strives for shock value to break the spell of our complacency and force us to own up to our quality responsibilities. It is tough to deny that we should focus on prevention and stop accepting defects as inevitable. Who could disagree that the world would be a better place to do business if things were done correctly the first time, saving the waste of scrap, rework, and customer dissatisfaction? And although Crosby's fourteen steps provide only minimal guidance for practical implementation, they encompass a lot of common sense.

Imai wants us to see the forest for the trees. He wants us to break from our preoccupation with gimmicks and isolated programs and understand that the underlying attitude of continuous improvement holds the key to success. Imai challenges the way we think about work; he sees improvement as a preoccupation of every person, every day. He tries to have us overcome our dependence on results management and value the process as much as the outcomes we seek. In many ways, Imai's work can be seen as an amplification of the continuous improvement theme so strongly advocated by Deming.

Deming's points go beyond principles of quality management: his attack is aimed squarely at the very heart of management as we know it in the West today. "Only transformation of the American style of management . . . can halt the decline and give American industry a chance to lead the world again" (p. x). More than any of the other quality leaders, Deming has developed a complete system of improvement that extends from his challenging philosophy of managerial thought and behavior to his evolution of the statistical quality control methods pioneered by Walter Shewhart in the 1920s. He rails against Crosby's "exhortations" to do things right the first time and argues that it is management's responsibility to first fix the system in which people work: "Exhortations and posters generate frustration and resentment. They advertise to the production worker that the management are unaware of the barriers to pride of workmanship" (p. 67). Although Deming's fourteen points and "system of profound knowledge" do not provide as clear an implementation path as many would like, his integration of the disparate disciplines of psychology, quality, statistics, and economics has been essential to furthering our understanding.

So which approach is right for you? There are obviously no simple answers. Praiseworthy experts and consultants abound who will tell you that Deming has the corner on truth and that all others are charlatans. But experience shows that no quality expert's approach or thinking can be adopted wholesale without modification to the company culture. Every organization has its own personality, language, and idiosyncrasies.

Trying to force a quality philosophy on an organization is like transplanting an organ from a donor with a different blood type: rejection is bound to come sooner or later.

Become familiar with the thinking of the experts, including others not detailed here: James Harrington, Bill Conway, and Dorian Shanin of the United States; Kaoru Ishikawa, Masao Nemoto, and Genichi Taguchi of Japan. Find an approach that feels right for you and your organization. Developing a quality philosophy is a learning process. Although you must have "constancy of purpose" in your quest for improvement, you have to learn what works well and what does not. Make the quality philosophy yours and not something read in a book or professed by a consultant. Phase 1 training provides a forum for executives to explore quality philosophies and to begin the process of articulating an approach that will most effectively reflect their values and aspirations.

REFERENCES

Allaire, P. A., and Rickard, N. E. "Quality and Participation at Xerox." *Journal for Quality and Participation*, Mar. 1989, pp. 24–26.

ASQC Quality Press and Quality Resources. *Quality Management Benchmark Assessment*. Milwaukee, Wis.: ASQC Quality Press, 1991.

Baatz, E. B. "The Changing Face of the Organization." *Electronic Business*, Mar. 18, 1991, pp. 60–64.

Bemowski, K. "Big Q at Big Blue." *Quality Progress*, May 1991, pp. 17–21.

Bemowski, K. "Carrying on the P&G Tradition." *Quality Progress*, May 1992, pp. 21–25.

Bersbach, P. L., and Wahl, P. R. "TQM Applied—Cradle to Grave." *Proceedings of the Third Annual Variability Reduction Symposium: Tools for Achieving Continuous Measurable Improvement*, May 1991, pp. 71–76.

Blauw, J. N., and During, W. E. "Total Quality Control in Dutch Industry." *Quality Progress*, Feb. 1990, pp. 50–52.

Block, P. *The Empowered Manager: Positive Political Skills at Work*. San Francisco: Jossey-Bass, 1991.

Brager, J. "The Customer-Focused Quality Leader." *Quality Progress*, May 1992, pp. 51–53.

Cantello, F. X., Chalmers, J. E., and Evans, J. E. "Evolution to an Effective and Enduring SPC System." *Quality Progress,* Feb. 1990, pp. 60–64.

Cocheu, T. *Training for Quality: INFO-LINE.* Alexandria, Va.: American Society for Training and Development, 1988.

Cocheu, T. "Training for Quality Improvement." *Training & Development,* Jan. 1989, pp. 56–62.

Cocheu, T. "Integrating Training with Quality Strategy." *Technical & Skills Training,* Feb.-Mar. 1992a, pp. 20–26.

Cocheu, T. "Training for Quality Improvement." *Design & Construction Quality Forum,* Winter 1992b, pp. 28–37.

Cocheu, T. "Training with Quality." *Training & Development,* May 1992c, pp. 23–32.

Compaq Computer Corporation. *World Class Supplier Process: Framework for Material Improvement.* Houston, Tex.: Compaq Computer Corporation, 1990.

Cornell, J. E., and Herman, S. M. "The Quality Difference." *Training & Development,* Aug. 1989, pp. 55–61.

Covey, S. R. *The Seven Habits of Highly Effective People.* New York: Simon & Schuster, 1989.

"The Cracks in Quality." *Economist,* Apr. 18, 1992, pp. 67–68.

Crosby, P. B. *Quality Is Free: The Art of Making Quality Certain.* New York: Mentor, 1979.

Crosby, P. B. *Quality Without Tears: The Art of Hassle-Free Management.* New York: McGraw-Hill, 1984.

de Geus, A. P. "Planning as Learning." *Harvard Business Review,* Mar.-Apr. 1988, pp. 70–74.

Deming, W. E. *Out of the Crisis.* Cambridge: Center for Advanced Engineering Study, Massachusetts Institute of Technology, 1982.

Ernst & Young. *International Quality Study.* Cleveland, Ohio: Ernst & Young, 1992.

Eureka, W. E., and Ryan, N. E. *The Customer-Driven Company: Managerial Perspectives on QFD.* Dearborn, Mich.: ASI Press, 1988.

Everett, M., and James, B. C. "Continuous Quality Improvement in Healthcare: A Perfect Fit." *Journal of Quality and Participation,* Jan.-Feb. 1991, pp. 10–14.

Federal Express Corporation. *Information Book.* Memphis, Tenn.: Federal Express Corporation, 1991.

Feigenbaum, A. V. *Total Quality Control.* New York: McGraw-Hill, 1983.

Fishman, N. "Our Customers Want Seamless Excellence in Their Training." *Journal for Quality and Participation,* Dec. 1990, pp. 24–27.

Galagan, P. A. "Donald E. Petersen, Chairman of Ford and Champion of Its People." *Training & Development,* Aug. 1988, pp. 20–24.

Galagan, P. A. "David T. Kearns: A CEO's View of Training." In American Society for Training and Development, *Corporate Case Studies: Strategic Use of Training.* Alexandria, Va.: American Society for Training and Development, 1991a.

Galagan, P. A. "How Wallace Changed Its Mind." *Training & Development,* June 1991b, pp. 23–28.

Gauntlet Group. *Organizational Excellence in the High Technology Industry.* Emeryville, Calif.: Gauntlet Group, 1991.

Geber, B. "The Resurrection of Ford." *Training,* Apr. 1989, pp. 23–32.

Gilbert, R. J. "Are You Committed or COMMITTED?" *Quality Progress,* May 1990, pp. 45–48.

Gill, M. S. "Stalking Six Sigma." *Business Month,* Jan. 1990, pp. 42–46.

Gitlow, H. S. *Planning for Quality, Productivity, & Competitive Position.* Homewood, Ill.: Dow Jones-Irwin, 1990.

GOAL/QPC Research Committee. *Hoshin Planning: A Planning System for Implementing Total Quality Management (TQM).* Research report no. 89-10-03. Methuen, Mass.: GOAL/QPC, 1989a.

GOAL/QPC Research Committee. *Vision 2000, America's Top 1,000 Companies' Quality Progress.* Research report no. 90-04-01. Methuen, Mass.: GOAL/QPC, 1989b.

Gordon, J. "Training Interview: Tom Peters." *Training,* June 1989, pp. 47–56.

Griffith, G. K. *Statistical Process Control for Long and Short Runs.* Milwaukee, Wis.: ASQC Quality Press, 1989.

Harrington, H. J. *Business Process Improvement.* New York: McGraw-Hill, sponsored by American Society for Quality Control, 1991.

Hauser, J. R., and Clausing, D. "The House of Quality." *Harvard Business Review,* May-June 1988, pp. 63–73.

Hudiburg, J. J. *Winning with Quality: The FLP Story.* White Plains, N.Y.: Quality Resources, 1991.

Imai, M. *Kaizen: The Key to Japan's Success.* New York: Random House, 1986.

International Standards Organization. *ISO 9004, Quality Management, and Quality System Elements: Guidelines.* Geneva, Switzerland: International Standards Organization, 1987.

Ishikawa, K. *What Is Quality Control?* Englewood Cliffs, N.J.: Prentice Hall, 1985.

Juran, J. M. *Managerial Breakthrough.* New York: McGraw-Hill, 1964.

Juran, J. M. "The Quality Trilogy." *Quality Process,* Aug. 1986, pp. 19–24.

Juran, J. M. *Juran on Leadership for Quality.* New York: Free Press, 1989.

Juran, J. M. *Total Quality Management—Magic Words or Hard Work: A View from the Real World.* Paper broadcast by Continuing Engineering Education Program, George Washington University, Washington, D.C., March 1992.

Kearns, D. T. "A Corporate Response." *Quality Progress,* Feb. 1988, pp. 28–30.

Kim, D. *Total Quality and System Dynamics: Complementary Approaches to Organizational Learning.* Paper no. E40-294. Cambridge: Sloan School of Management, Massachusetts Institute of Technology, 1990.

King, B. *Hoshin Planning: The Developmental Approach.* Methuen, Mass.: GOAL/QPC, 1989.

Klusman, C. J. "Total Quality Commitment at Boeing Military Airplanes: Taking a Quality Company Higher." *Journal for Quality and Participation,* Mar. 1989, pp. 32–36.

Kouzes, J. M., and Posner, B. Z. *The Leadership Challenge: How to Get Extraordinary Things Done in Organizations.* San Francisco: Jossey-Bass, 1987.

"Labor Letter." *Wall Street Journal,* Oct. 3, 1989, p. A1.

Labovitz, G. H., and Chang, Y. S. "Learn from the Best." *Quality Progress,* May 1990, pp. 81–85.

LeBoeuf, M. *The Greatest Management Principle in the World.* New York: Putnam, 1985.

Levinson, H. J., and DeHont, C. "Leading to Quality." *Quality Progress,* May 1992, pp. 55–60.

Lofgren, G. Q. "Quality System Registration." *Quality Progress,* May 1991, pp. 35–37.

Mann, R. W., and Staudenmier, J. M. "Strategic Shifts in Executive Development." *Training & Development,* July 1991, pp. 37–40.

March, A. *A Note on Quality: The Views of Deming, Juran, and Crosby.* Paper no. 9-687-011. Cambridge, Mass.: Harvard Business School, Harvard University, 1990.

Mizuno, S. *Management for Quality Improvement: The Seven New QC Tools.* Cambridge, Mass.: Productivity Press, 1988. (English translation.)

Motorola University. *Supplier/Customer Training: A Proven Partnership in Quality.* Schaumburg, Ill.: Motorola, 1990.

Naisbitt, J., and Aburdene, P. *Reinventing the Corporation: Transforming Your Job and Company for the New Information Society.* New York: Warner Books, 1985.

National Institute of Standards and Technology. *1991 Application Guidelines, Malcolm Baldrige National Quality Award.* Gaithersburg, Md.: National Institute of Standards and Technology, 1990.

National Institute of Standards and Technology. *1992 Award Criteria, Malcolm Baldrige National Quality Award.* Gaithersburg, Md.: National Institute of Standards and Technology, 1991.

Peach, R. W. "Creating a Pattern of Excellence." *Target,* Winter 1990, pp. 15–22.

Peters, T. *Thriving on Chaos: A Handbook for a Management Revolution.* New York: Knopf, 1988.

Peters, T. "Making It Happen." *Journal of Quality and Participation,* Mar. 1989, pp. 6–13.

Phillips, W. L., Chang, D. R., and Buzzell, R. D. "Product Quality, Cost Position, and Business Performance." *Journal of Marketing,* 1983, *47,* 26–43.

ReVelle, J. B. "The Tools of Total Quality Management (TQM)." *Quality Management Forum,* 1991, *17*(4), 1–3.

Ross, P. J. *Taguchi Techniques for Quality Engineering.* New York: McGraw-Hill, 1988.

Schaffer, R., and Thompson, H. "Successful Change Programs Begin with Results." *Harvard Business Review,* Jan.-Feb. 1992, pp. 80–89.

Senge, P. M. *The Fifth Discipline: The Art and Practice of the Learning Organization.* New York: Doubleday/Currency, 1990a.

Senge, P. M. "The Leader's New Work: Building Learning Organizations." *Sloan Management Review,* Fall 1990b, pp. 7–23.

Smith, F. W. "The Human Side of Quality." *Quality Progress,* Oct. 1990, pp. 19–21.

Stratton, B. "A Forum for the Power of Quality." *Quality Progress,* Feb. 1990a, pp. 19–24.

Stratton, B. "What Makes It Take? What Makes It Break?" *Quality Progress,* Apr. 1990b, pp. 14–18.

U.S. General Accounting Office. *U.S. Companies Improve Performance Through Quality Efforts.* Washington, D.C.: Government Printing Office, 1991.

Van Nuland, Y. "Prerequisites to Implementation." *Quality Progress,* June 1990, pp. 36–39.

Varian, T. "Communicating Total Quality Inside the Organization." *Quality Progress,* June 1991, pp. 30–31.

INDEX

193